also by Romney Steele
My Nepenthe

plum gorgeous

plum gorgeous

ROMNEY STEELE

Recipes and Memories from the Orchard

For Rosa ♥ — Enjoy!
on her birthday.

photography by
Sara Remington

Romney Steele

July 21, 2011

**Andrews McMeel
Publishing, LLC**

Kansas City · Sydney · London

Andrews McMeel Publishing, LLC
an Andrews McMeel Universal company
1130 Walnut Street, Kansas City, Missouri 64106

www.andrewsmcmeel.com

11 12 13 14 15 SDB 10 9 8 7 6 5 4 3 2 1
ISBN: 978-1-4494-0240-2
Library of Congress Control Number: 2010937868

Design: Lisa Berman
Photography: Sara Remington
Food styled by the author
Painting by Trevor Hudson page 107, and Zachariah Hudson page 94
Line drawings by the author, except cake page 113 by Nicoya Hudson; bird page 94 and flourishes by Lisa Berman

www.romneysteele.com / www.mynepenthebook.com

ATTENTION: SCHOOLS AND BUSINESSES
Andrews McMeel books are available at quantity discounts with bulk purchase for educational, business, or sales promotional use. For information, please e-mail the Andrews McMeel Publishing Special Sales Department: specialsales@amuniversal.com

With love,

to Kate and to my sister Sara,
who shared the joys and sorrows of time and place

to Trevor, Nicoya, Isabella, and Sumner,
the "little ones" that this book reminisces

and to Elena, who taught me what to do
when faced with a glut of gorgeous fruit

To be happy you must have taken the measure of your powers,
tasted the fruits of your passion, and learned your place in the world.

–George Santayana

a gate at the window

The seed for this book first came to me years ago, on a drive south along the California coast from Big Sur to Santa Barbara with my friend and gardener Kate Healey. Together, we were always dreaming and talking about food, whether about the events we collaborated on professionally or a recipe or preserve we might make with all the fruit and vegetables she was growing in her garden and orchard—the one I would eventually live at. The warmth of Kate's English-style country kitchen with its jumbled shelves chock-full of home-canned tomatoes and preserved fruits became my home away from home, where I tended my young children and shared a great many meals and jam sessions. It is really because of her and her family that I have a story to write in the first place.

Back then, it was a delicate balance of dreaming about writing and doing the daily work that life on a mountaintop demands, along with working and caring for a family. I'm not sure that I was always good at it, but I will say that I loved working with beautiful fruit—the bought, gathered, and given—and still do. My earlier travels and experiences engaging with nature's bounty—whether picking grapes in France, living in the tropics surrounded by exotic fruit flavors, or in orchards closer to home—have always influenced my writing and cooking and are really at the heart of this book.

In putting *Plum Gorgeous* together I discovered that I'm not one to simply write a cookbook in the traditional manner. For me there is always something more that is necessary and true, an artistic drive and curiosity beyond the plate that can't be denied. It's the story, imaginary and actual, that I'm after—the memories, dreams, places, and poetry that come with the journey. The stirring of a pot of rosy colored raspberries with rose petals and sugar matters not only for what it becomes—a lovely jam—but also for the story it unfolds and reveals.

One evening, more recently, while at my sister's home out in the country working on this book, she had a delightful longtime friend over who asked about my Blenheim apricot jam—she literally swooned and fluttered over it. How was it I maintained that golden amber color, she begged. The discussion turned to Meyer lemon curd, and how each year she makes it, using only egg yolks, for the nuns at the mission. There is no sin in eating something so delicious and rich, she cried out with obvious pleasure. By this time we were drinking wine and nibbling on the last of the kumquat and couscous salad—just photographed for the book—under the shade of a grapefruit tree in the garden as the sun went down, and lavishing spoonfuls of rose petal jam onto toast with runny cheese for dessert. Bunny's food memories stretching across the globe were only getting more generous, and we were delirious with laughter. I thought to myself, this is exactly what this book is about—this moment, this food, and what is unfolding now.

Plum Gorgeous is surely a book about the sensuous and enchanting nature of fruit and what to do with it in the kitchen. But more than that, it's about the pleasures and joys of the table: my own "longing for a touchstone" and a place to return to; the memories, maps, and connections that abound around each recipe; and the stories and tales that come with each. A delicious outcome is enhanced by the time spent in the kitchen chopping and putting together a painter's salad of peaches and heirloom tomatoes with burrata cheese, and the spontaneous gatherings around the table that follow. It's recognizing the gorgeousness that food, and particularly fruit, can be all on its own.

Food keeps us fed and nourished, so why not have it be gorgeous and ecstatic too? For me it's so important that food is beautiful, that it not only looks ravishing on the plate, but that it is also delicious and encourages tasting with all the senses. What I love both about cooking and making books, and have tried to illustrate in *Plum Gorgeous,* is the creative process inherent in both and how they play off each other. I take great pleasure in how Sara Remington's photographs so intimately and beautifully capture a sense of place and inspire a feeling of magic and romance.

That said, this book is very much a cookbook and definitely about fruits and the seasons in which each grows. It has recipes that are written in the traditional way and, like other cookbooks, hopes to inspire and engage you in the cooking process. For the most part,

I believe recipes are just guides; they are a good place to start and I very much encourage you to play with your fruit. Look for fruit that comes from a local farm, if not from a neighbor or a friendly orchard; ask about its province, its story. You'll be surprised at what you learn and at how that translates into what you make with it.

I adore pure flavors, distilling an idea or recipe, and in this case a fruit, down to its essence—so don't expect to find a lot of fancy pairings, or heavily sweetened, multi-step desserts, or even challenging savory dishes. Use your imagination; feel free to substitute one fruit for another. For example, try making my Pink Grapefruit Cassis Granita (page 29) with blood orange juice and Champagne. It's divine. Substitute just-picked blackberries for the plums in the Plum Gorgeous Almond Tart (page 122), or make it with French prunes that arrive later in the season, doused in brandy first. Be flexible and try something different, as the orchard and seasons often demand. Be willing to make mistakes; it's how you will learn and develop your own palate and taste preferences.

Some of these recipes are inspired by the time I spent at Kate's orchard and worked in a professional kitchen, but are now adapted for home. Others are inspired by my travels, books I've read, and chefs I admire. All of them strive to be fruit forward and flavorful, so starting with a quality, seasonal product is paramount. For me cooking is like love: Find the heart in the moment that sings and nurture it. Let the fruit speak for itself.

My uncle, artist Kaffe Fassett, and his glorious books on the art of knitting, quilting, and mosaic-making have inspired my own creative process, as a cook and a writer, and this book in particular. Spending a day with Kaffe is a revelation in color, in imagination, and in dreaming beyond the painter's palette; eating with him and cooking for him is one more level of immersion in a sensual world.

I hope my own passion for the seductive colors, textures, shapes, and flavors of select fruits and the playful memories and reminisces surrounding my year living at a Big Sur orchard come across in this book and in these recipes and inspire your own enthusiasm for cooking with fruit, if only just a little.

Longing for a touchstone—a land where life stood still and my memories could be relived.

—David Mas Masumoto, *Epitaph for a Peach*

The Oranges of the Island are like blazing fire
Amongst the emerald boughs
And the lemons are like the paleness of a lover
Who has spent the night crying

—Abd al-Rahman ibn Abi al-'Abbas

1

oranges
of memory
and Other Citrus

citrus

Oranges remind me of the thick-cut, dark, amber marmalade my friend Kate makes each year with fruit from her trees, and eating the candied goodness on toast while drinking strong cups of milky English tea in her kitchen. The Seville bitter oranges from the south of Spain that first arrived in the Mediterranean via the Moors, the variety aficionados say make the best marmalade, are what I seek out in January when I make my own. Citrus groves also abound in southern Italy and in many great Arab palaces, and come to mind when I think of the flavors from these countries: ruby wheels sprinkled with cinnamon and orange blossom water in Morocco; tangerine or kumquat paired with dates in a couscous salad; and spiced preserved lemons added to rice and meat dishes. Sicilians make a sweet orange sauce for fish, a recipe I've adapted here for marmalade chicken. Both the Italians and the Spanish use the zest and flesh of oranges and lemons for stuffing oily sardines, but you can simply scatter the fragrant zest over the top of the fish as it comes off the grill. Early Chinese documents mention oranges being held in the hand so that the warmth releases their scent. It's hard to imagine a more lovely visual.

Consider the lemon for its bracing juice and fragrant zest, adding zing to both sweet and savory dishes all year long. It is the go-to fruit for refreshing lemonade with lavender, a homey Bundt cake, or a tart curd. Meyer lemons, a sweeter, thin-skinned hybrid, are popular in California. They can be grown in a pot and fed with the occasional dose of coffee grounds for good health. Verdant limes add vibrancy to spicy foods, grilled shrimp, and tropical dishes, as do pink grapefruit to an icy granita or paired with other citrus in a compote. Candy the peel of most any citrus and dip the ends in chocolate for a special after-dinner treat.

meyer lemon curd

Lemon curd is my "when life gives you lemons" riposte, especially when it comes to Meyer lemons, the sweeter hybrid citrus beloved by Californians. I adore making it and having it on hand for filling cakes and tartlets, or simply to serve with scones at teatime. It's also a great starting point for other desserts: Fold in softly whipped cream and use as a base for a gratin, such as my Blueberry Lemon-Lime Gratin (page 9). You can make curd with just about any fruit, but a classic tart curd made with good-quality lemons is my favorite. For a sweeter curd, or if using standard lemons such as Eureka, add up to 3 tablespoons more sugar per cup of juice. Passion fruit and raspberry also make popular curds.

MAKES ABOUT 2 CUPS

2 eggs plus 4 yolks

Scant 1 cup sugar

Finely grated zest from
2 organic Meyer lemons

1 cup fresh lemon juice
(from 4 to 5 large Meyer
lemons or standard lemons)

¼ cup (½ stick) cold butter,
cut into pieces

Whisk the eggs and sugar in a medium heatproof bowl, then whisk in the zest and juice. Place the bowl over a gently simmering pot of water and continuously stir with a wooden spoon until it begins to thicken, about 5 minutes. Stir in the butter; cook, stirring frequently, until the curd coats the back of the spoon, about 5 minutes more.

Pour the curd into a separate bowl. Press a piece of plastic wrap on the surface while cooling to prevent a skin from forming. The curd will keep for up to 4 weeks in the refrigerator, and a year in the freezer. You can also pot in sterilized jars. Follow manufacturer's instructions for proper sealing.

NOTE: For lemon-lime curd, use an equal blend of lemon and lime juice and add 1 to 2 tablespoons sugar. For orange and/or tangerine curd, start with less sugar, adding more to taste, plus a little fresh lemon juice to help set the curd and balance flavor.

honey
lavender
lemonade

There's nothing like fresh-squeezed lemonade on a hot day in the garden, and it's one of the best reasons to have your own lemon tree. We always make our own lemonade, keeping a pitcher of it in the fridge. Lavender flowers add a pleasing, floral note–try fresh thyme or mint, as well.

½ cup light honey

¼ cup sugar

Pinch lavender flowers

Zest from 2 lemons

Fresh lemon juice

Lavender or mint sprigs,
  for garnish

Lemon rounds (optional)

Gently heat the honey, sugar, lavender, lemon zest, and ½ cup water and simmer for 1 to 2 minutes. Remove from the heat, cover, and steep for 20 minutes. Pour the syrup (straining if you want a lighter herbal flavor) into a glass jar, cover, and chill. You should end up with about 1 cup lavender syrup; it will keep in the refrigerator indefinitely.

For a generous 1 quart lemonade, combine ½ cup lavender syrup, ½ cup fresh lemon juice, and about 4 cups water in a glass pitcher. Stir well and pour over tall glasses of ice. Garnish with sprigs of lavender or fresh mint.

For a lemon spritzer, pour about 1 ounce lavender syrup over a tall glass of ice along with a few squeezes of fresh lemon juice, to taste. Top with sparkling water or spirits; garnish with lemon rounds.

Lemons make me happy, seeing them on my table in a Moroccan bowl with turquoise edging. The shiny ovals remind me of living at Henry Miller's house, the jumbled oasis down the hill from the orchard, the sturdy redwood table at the center of the room where I would always place that bowl and fill it with lemons from the tree. My ode to joy.

*B*lueberries and citrus have a delicious affinity for each other and are lovely in this simple fruit gratin. It's a relatively foolproof dessert and yet noteworthy enough to serve at a dinner party. To achieve the caramelizing affect, it's best if you have a kitchen torch, but don't despair if not. You can just place the dish under a broiler or in a very hot oven, on the top shelf, for a couple of minutes. You don't want the berries to fully cook through, but to be warm without being mushy.

blueberry lemon-lime gratin

SERVES 4 TO 6

2 cups fresh blueberries

½ cup Blueberry Sauce (page 120)

½ cup whipping cream, lightly whipped

1 cup lemon-lime curd (see Note at Meyer Lemon Curd recipe on page 5)

Sugar for caramelizing

Toss the blueberries with a little of the syrup in a medium bowl and let macerate for 15 minutes. Divide the berries among individual gratin dishes along with some of the syrup, or spoon into one larger gratin dish. Fold the whipped cream into the lemon-lime curd, and then pour over the berries. Scatter a tablespoon or so of sugar over the top of each gratin and caramelize with a kitchen torch, until golden and the berries are warmed through.

But there better not be anybody with you when I arrive–no creamy lemon voices, no southern drawl, no honey business.

–Henry Miller to Anaïs Nin, *A Literate Passion: Letters of Anaïs Nin and Henry Miller*

honey-basil tangerine compote

A simple compote of marinated citrus segments with a hint of basil is alluring all on its own. Yet it can be dressed up with slices of pineapple and a sprinkling of toasted coconut for a tropical version, and a few cookies on the side, or served with sorbet or ice cream. It also makes a nice accompaniment to my Lemon Almond Cake (page 38) made with orange zest instead of lemon. For a boozier compote, stir in a little brandy along with the flower water.

SERVES 4

4 to 5 honey tangerines

1 tablespoon honey

1 to 2 tablespoons sugar

½ vanilla bean, cut lengthwise, with seeds

Few basil leaves

1 tablespoon orange flower water

Remove the peel and pith from the tangerines by cutting around the perimeter of the fruit using a very sharp knife. Working over a glass bowl to capture any escaped juices, cut out individual segments of tangerine (*supremes*), removing the seeds as you go. Squeeze the remaining membrane over a sieve to strain any juice into a small saucepot, then add the juice from the bowl. You should have a minimum of ½ cup juice, or a little more.

Add the honey, sugar to taste, vanilla seeds and pod, and basil leaves to the juice and bring to a simmer. Cook for 5 minutes, until lightly syrupy. Pour over the *supremes* and stir in the orange flower water. Macerate for at least 1 hour, or longer. Chill to serve.

The honey tangerine, also known as Murcott orange after the Florida nursery owner who first developed the variety, is a cross between the sweet orange and tangerine, with rich, orange flesh that is typically quite sweet. California Murcotts, also known as Delite mandarins, are in fact very different from their Florida cousins, which tend to have more seeds and less range in flavor. I prefer California Murcotts for their delicate quality and taste—excellent for eating out of hand—but either works well in this compote.

Apple green windowsills. The color orange against a backdrop
of sea and sky. Vermilion flowers on a wall, as if in Mexico.
Flirtatious tiles. Girl's moment in the sun. This was the
house where I began to love again. Where my kids had
a lemon yellow room, like morning sunshine.

These classic French butter cookies are the perfect sweet for afternoon coffee, and are also just right served alongside a cooked custard or fruit compote. The dough keeps well in the freezer, so you can simply bake what you need at the last minute. You can also roll out the (unfrozen) dough and cut into shapes, or use as a base for a fruit tart. For miniature cookie sandwiches, fill the baked and cooled sables with citrus curd (see Note to Meyer Lemon Curd, page 5).

orange pistachio sables

MAKES ABOUT 2 DOZEN

½ cup (1 stick) butter, at room temperature

¼ cup confectioners' sugar

2 teaspoons finely grated orange zest

1 egg yolk

2 teaspoons orange flower water

1 cup flour

⅓ cup pistachios or almonds, finely ground

Pinch ground cardamom

Pinch salt

Demerara sugar or other sanding sugar, for coating

Preheat the oven to 350°F.

Beat the butter with the confectioners' sugar and zest in a medium bowl or stand mixer until light and fluffy, about 5 minutes. Beat in the egg yolk and orange flower water. Stir together the flour, ground nuts, cardamom, and salt. Add the flour mixture to the sugar mixture and beat until just blended.

Transfer the dough to a lightly floured board (or use confectioners' sugar on the board) and gently bring together in a ball. Roll the dough into a cylinder about 1½ inches thick, or larger depending on the size cookies you want, then roll in the sanding sugar. Wrap in plastic and freeze for at least 1 hour.

Slice the dough into ¼-inch-thick rounds and place on a parchment-lined baking sheet. Bake for 7 to 10 minutes, until golden.

Winter on the mountain cultivates growth and change below thick mulch and soggy retreat. There are running gullies of mud and heavy rain, along with new tasks required merely to stay dry. Vividness endures despite what is true with azure days and unexpected sunshine, when all that seemed wrong feels suddenly right. The emerald sea beyond is at times surreal, a steady backdrop against melancholic skies and sturdy oaks, bearing dramatic views at daybreak. Night knocks early and we tumble into one bed, tired and grateful for refuge, the mornings arriving even earlier, with a new rush to school, and down the hill we go. I am at once discontent and comforted by the coziness of home, the robust but thinning redwood walls, a potbelly stove, and a sunken tub just off the galley—we cook, bathe, draw, and sleep within range of each other, closeness being at once beautiful and a challenge, heartbreaking and poetic. A bowl of cloudless lemons at my table perfumes the room; the turquoise vase spills over with the fiery glow of heart-shaped persimmon and Persephone's pomegranate. We light the room with candles, sometimes out of necessity, cheer ourselves with mugs of sweet tea and toast with candied marmalade on rainy afternoons, and set ourselves up to paint. I relish my friends to draw us near; nothing is better than cheap French wine in tumblers to share over a bowl of warming soup. Tonight it's just the three of us, anticipating dawn, the sweet smell of orange blossoms in spring.

Branches of orange,
lovely with flower.
Seven are the

I *have made orange marmalade almost every year since I lived at Kate's*
orchard, but hers, made with Seville oranges from her tree, remains a personal
favorite. Both her English grandmother and aunt made marmalade, and they are
the people to whom Kate credits her interest. In the 1950s, her aunt Eileen used
to make it on her farm in Uruguay for BOAC, the British state airlines. This is
Kate's recipe, in her own words:

kate's
orange
marmalade

I use Sevilles when my tree produces enough, or Valencias or navels depending
on what is happening in the orchard. First scrub them and make sure there are no
blemishes, bugs, or filth.

For one batch of my marmalade, take a 10- to 11-quart stainless pot and put in
about a dozen or so organic oranges, scrubbed clean. When all the oranges and
approximately 4 lemons are in the pot, cover them with boiling water. Place the lid
on, and simmer until the fruit is tender—this can take up to 3 hours. You can test the
fruit by poking it with a sharp knife or skewer; if it goes in easily, it's ready. Let the
fruit cool in the water overnight.

The next day, remove one orange or lemon at a time and chop on a cutting board
into thin or thick slices (I have a wooden board that is slanted so the juices don't run
away). The important thing is to save all the juices (in the pot and on the board) and
pick out all the seeds as you go. Add the chopped fruit back into the pot and bring
back to a simmer. Add sugar in equal parts. My way is to estimate the height of the
fruit in the pot; if it is 3 inches deep then I add 3 inches of sugar and simmer until
dissolved. The longer you simmer, the darker the marmalade. I like to let it sit for a
day or longer before I put it into jars. I do think this improves the flavor.

I have always enjoyed reading
recipes from tattered old
cookbooks or recipe cards
with copperplate handwriting
that have been passed down
through the years. The old
recipes often are without
exact measurements or
amounts . . . my style exactly.

–Kate Healey

marmalade chicken

This is a homey roasted orange chicken that is both sweet and savory. For a sweeter version, use more marmalade or add a pinch of sugar to the saucepot towards the end. Roasting orange wedges alongside the chicken adds a nice touch and is tasty besides. Serve with saffron-scented rice.

SERVES 4 TO 6

1 (3½- to 4-pound) chicken, cut into 8 pieces

Salt and freshly ground black pepper

Juice of 2 oranges

Juice of 1 lemon

2 cloves garlic, chopped

6 tablespoons Kate's Orange Marmalade (page 17)

1 onion, halved and sliced

Olive oil

⅓ cup coarsely chopped cilantro or parsley, plus more for garnish

Balsamic vinegar

Preheat the oven to 375°F.

Place the chicken in a shallow dish and season all over with salt and pepper. Whisk the orange and lemon juice, garlic, and 4 tablespoons of the marmalade in a small bowl; pour over the chicken. Cover and refrigerate for at least 1 hour, turning the chicken over halfway through so it is well coated on both sides.

Scatter the onion on the bottom of a glass baking dish or medium casserole. Place the chicken pieces on top and pour the marinade over. Drizzle with a little olive oil and scatter with the chopped herbs. Bake for about 45 minutes, occasionally spooning the juices over the chicken as it cooks, until the thigh juices run clear when pierced with a fork. Transfer the chicken and onion to a platter and loosely cover with foil.

Pour off some of the pan juices into a small saucepot and stir in the remaining 2 tablespoons marmalade and a splash of balsamic vinegar. Bring to a simmer over medium heat; cook until it is slightly reduced and syrupy, about 5 minutes. Pour over the chicken and scatter with more fresh herbs to serve.

Inspired by the flavors of Morocco, this salad literally came together on the plate—the colors and textures too gorgeous to ignore. Cara Cara oranges are early- to mid-season red navels, with a distinctive sweet flavor and color all their own. Blood oranges or a combination of oranges and tangerines would be similarly ravishing. If you can't find radish greens, use other microgreens or scatter with fresh cilantro leaves.

To make the dressing, whisk together the olive oil, orange juice, flower water, vinegar, cumin, cinnamon, and cayenne in a small bowl. Season with salt and pepper.

To assemble the salad, arrange the orange slices on a platter or individual plates. Scatter with the onion, pomegranate seeds, basil, and radish greens. Drizzle with the dressing and serve.

*And she feeds you tea and oranges
that come all the way from China.*

−Leonard Cohen, from "Suzanne"

moroccan orange salad

SERVES 4 TO 6

Dressing
⅓ cup extra virgin olive oil

3 tablespoons fresh orange juice

2 teaspoons orange flower water

Splash sherry vinegar

½ teaspoon cumin seed,
toasted and ground

Pinch cinnamon

Dash cayenne pepper

Salt and freshly ground
black pepper

Salad
4 to 6 Cara Cara or blood oranges,
peeled and sliced

1 small red onion, thinly sliced

½ cup pomegranate seeds

Small handful opal basil leaves

Radish microgreens

preserved lemons

Preserved lemon is a common North African condiment and something I learned to make from my stepmother, Elena, who grew up in the Mediterranean. The lemons are traditionally quartered partway, leaving the stem intact, then stuffed with salt and covered with lemon juice to preserve. Over the years, I have taken to cutting the lemons all the way through (or occasionally slicing into rounds, as in the alternate method below) and instead layering the salt and spices. Either way, it takes a good 3 weeks or longer for them to cure. Slivers of salty rind are delicious stirred through couscous, beans, and grains or added to olives. Chopped, they add a zing to dressings, gremolata (see Grilled Sardines with Preserved Lemon Gremolata, page 24), and meaty dishes.

MAKES 1 QUART

8 organic or unsprayed lemons, preferably thin-skinned

Kosher salt or coarse sea salt

1 or 2 bay leaves

1 cinnamon stick

1 dried chile, crushed or whole

½ teaspoon black peppercorns

Fresh lemon juice

Olive oil

Wash the lemons well and pat dry. Quarter lengthwise and toss vigorously in a bowl with about ½ cup salt to coat. Pack the lemons tightly in a sterilized quart jar, layering as you go with the bay leaves, cinnamon, chile, peppercorns, and any residual salt and juice.

Add enough lemon juice to fill about half the jar. Cover and set aside in a warm place. Shake once a day or so for 3 days, to help release the juices. Add more lemon juice, this time enough to fully cover the lemons. This is very important. Pour a thin slick of olive oil over the top. If you like, you can also place a round of parchment on top, to help keep the lemons submerged.

Cover and place in a dark cupboard or cool area of the kitchen. They are usually ready in about a month—the rinds will be quite tender and the salt completely dissolved—sometimes a little longer. They usually get better with age.

quick pickled lemons

This method tends to be a little more immediate, and the way I used to make them quite frequently, with great success. The lemons do absorb more salt this way, so use sparingly. I like these for when I want to use both the flesh and rind of the lemon in a dish, or to scatter the pretty rounds on fish as it bakes.

Slice scrubbed lemons into rounds, then layer in a sterilized jar with a light sprinkling of salt, torn pieces of hot chile pepper (like arbol), and bay leaves. Weight the lemons if possible, or press down with the back of a wooden spoon to release some of their juice. Cover with more fresh lemon juice and pour a slick of extra virgin olive oil over the top. They can be used almost immediately, but are best after about 2 weeks.

grilled sardines
with preserved lemon gremolata

*S*avor the flavors of the Mediterranean in late summer, when sardines are plentiful and enjoying a meal al fresco is a must. It's best to enjoy these oily little fish with your fingers, removing the bones as you eat and not giving a darn about how you might look in the process.

Gremolata is an Italian condiment typically made with lemon zest, garlic, and parsley; the cilantro and preserved lemon here give it added zeal. Made without the currants and bread crumbs, it is delicious on steak.

SERVES 4 TO 6

1½ to 2 pounds fresh sardines, cleaned and gutted

Sea salt and freshly ground black pepper

Preserved Lemon Gremolata

Leaves from ½ bunch parsley, coarsely chopped

Leaves from ½ bunch cilantro, coarsely chopped

½ cup toasted coarse bread crumbs

2 pieces Preserved Lemons (page 22), finely diced

3 tablespoons currants, plumped in hot water

2 cloves garlic, minced

1 shallot, finely chopped

Finely grated zest of 1 lemon

Olive oil, for drizzling and brushing

Season the sardines on both sides with salt and pepper. Leave at room temperature while you prepare the gremolata.

To make the gremolata, combine the herbs, bread crumbs, preserved lemon, currants, garlic, shallot, and lemon zest in a small bowl. Drizzle with olive oil, just enough to moisten.

Heat a grill pan or outdoor grill to medium-hot. Brush the sardines on both sides with olive oil. Grill for 2 to 3 minutes per side, until just cooked through. Arrange on a platter and scatter with the gremolata. Grind fresh black pepper over the top and serve.

of sea and sky. Vermilion flowe

- lemona
- lemon
- a bowl
- lemon
- lemons

a wall, as if in Mexico. Flirtatio

ranita is a refreshing and playful alternative to sorbet, more like an ice, and the blush juice of pink grapefruit makes a particularly pretty one. Make the same day you plan to serve it. Before juicing the grapefruit, remove as much peel as you think you might like to candy. Along with the candied peel, serve the granita with fresh grapefruit segments, lightly macerated in sugar and Prosecco.

pink grapefruit cassis granita

SERVES 4 TO 6

3 cups fresh ruby grapefruit juice
(from about 6 grapefruits)

½ cup sugar

Cassis

Candied Grapefruit Peel
(recipe below)

Bring 1 cup of the juice and the sugar to a simmer over low heat, stirring, until the sugar is dissolved. Pour in the remaining 2 cups juice and stir in cassis to taste. Chill thoroughly.

Pour the granita base into a shallow baking pan and place in the freezer. Stir every 15 minutes, until large ice crystals form, about 1 hour. Serve the granita in glass dessert bowls, garnished with candied grapefruit.

candied grapefruit peel

You can use this method for just about any citrus, paying attention to the various kinds of fruit and their inherent shape, as well as how bitter the pith is. For the candied citron pictured on page 27, for example, slice the fingers of a Buddha's hand fruit into thin rounds–do not scrape away any pith–and proceed to blanch, then cook in sugar syrup.

For candied grapefruit, scrape off most of the white pith from the peel. Slice the peel into desired size of strips or other shapes. Place in a small saucepot and cover with cool water. Bring to a boil and simmer for 2 minutes. Drain and refresh with cool water. Do this two more times. The third time, boil the peel for 15 minutes, until tender. Drain.

Return the peel to the pot and add water and sugar (½ cup water for every 1 cup sugar), enough to make a syrup that will generously cover the peel as it cooks. Cook over low heat until the peel is translucent, 20 to 30 minutes. Transfer the pieces to a rack to drain, reserving the syrup. While still warm, roll the pieces in sugar, using the tines of a fork. Cool completely, then store the candied peel between layers of parchment paper in an airtight container. It will keep for several weeks on the shelf, or indefinitely in the refrigerator. Use the syrup to flavor drinks, or for drizzling.

kumquats and toasted couscous with halloumi

This unusual salad, which came to me on a whim one day, combines some of my favorite foods. Halloumi is a traditional Cypriot cheese, popular also throughout the Middle East, and is commonly fried and sprinkled with mint. It's made from either goat or sheep milk or sometimes both and can be quite salty depending on the brand. It works beautifully in this room temperature dish, while the kumquats add a splash of sunshine to the earthy flavors.

SERVES 4 TO 6

Couscous

1 cup couscous

Pinch ground cinnamon

Pinch salt

About 1 teaspoon olive oil

Scant 1 cup boiling water

Dressing

⅓ cup extra virgin olive oil

1 teaspoon finely grated lemon zest

2 tablespoons fresh lemon or lime juice

Splash red wine vinegar

1 shallot, finely chopped

½ teaspoon coriander seed, toasted and coarsely ground

2 teaspoons chopped mint (optional)

Salt and freshly ground black pepper

Salad

8 ounces halloumi cheese, sliced into rounds

Olive oil

Chopped mint (optional)

8 kumquats, thinly sliced

6 dates, pitted and thinly sliced

½ cup parsley leaves

½ cup almonds, lightly toasted and coarsely chopped

To prepare the couscous, toast in a skillet with the cinnamon over low heat until fragrant and lightly browned, about 5 minutes. Transfer to a bowl. Add the salt and olive oil. Pour the boiling water over the top. Stir and cover; let sit for 15 minutes. Fluff with a fork before using.

To make the dressing, whisk together the olive oil, lemon zest and juice, vinegar, shallot, and coriander in a small bowl. Stir in the mint, if using, and season with salt and pepper.

To assemble the salad, fry the halloumi in a small skillet over medium-high heat in a small amount of olive oil, just enough to wet the pan. Turn to brown both sides. Transfer the cheese to plates and sprinkle with a little mint, if desired.

Toss the couscous with about half of the dressing. (You may have a little more couscous than you need. Determine for yourself how much couscous you want for each serving.) Stir in the kumquats, dates, and parsley. Top the cheese on the plates with the couscous mix. Scatter with the almonds and drizzle with more dressing as desired.

Use your fingers when eating these lime-dusted prawns, savoring every morsel with gusto. Look for spot prawns or large shrimp, preferably with the heads on. The aioli will keep in the refrigerator for about a week.

grilled
lime prawns
with aioli

SERVES 3 TO 4

Aioli
1 clove garlic, smashed

Pinch salt

2 egg yolks

1 cup olive oil

2 teaspoons finely grated lime zest

Fresh lime juice

Prawns
1½ to 2 pounds prawns,
with heads on

Sea salt and freshly
ground black pepper

Juice and finely grated zest of
2 limes, plus lime wedges
for serving

Olive oil, for drizzling

To make the aioli, place the garlic in a ceramic or wooden bowl with a pinch of salt and mash to a smooth paste with a pestle. Beat in the egg yolks. Gradually add the olive oil, continuing to beat with the pestle, until a thick puree forms. Stir in the lime zest, and add juice to taste. Add more salt, diluted with a little warm water, if needed. The aioli can also be made in a food processor.

To prepare the prawns, rinse and pat dry, but don't remove the heads. Thread a wooden skewer through the tail end to the head so that each prawn stands straight like a soldier. Place in a shallow dish and season both sides with salt and pepper. Sprinkle with the lime zest and squeeze fresh lime juice over the top. Drizzle with olive oil.

Heat a grill pan or outdoor grill to medium heat. If using a grill pan, brush a little oil on its surface as it heats. Grill the prawns until opaque in the center, about 2 minutes per side. Serve with the aioli and fresh limes on the side for squeezing.

rangpur lime mascarpone tart

angpur limes aren't really limes, but a cross between the mandarin and lemon, with orange flesh and skin. Their tart, almost tropical-like flavor brightens this simple cheese tart. If you can't find Rangpur limes, use a blend of fresh lime and tangerine juice. Caramelizing the top after it comes out of the oven adds a welcome burnt note and gives it a lovely finish besides. Serve with strawberry sauce (page 120), a dollop of thick cream or yogurt, and fresh passion fruit.

MAKES ONE 9- OR 10-INCH TART

½ recipe Sable Dough (page 122)

½ cup mascarpone cheese, at room temperature

½ cup sugar, plus more for caramelizing

2 eggs

2 teaspoons finely grated rangpur lime zest

½ cup fresh Rangpur lime juice

1 teaspoon pure vanilla extract

½ cup whipping cream

Roll out the dough and press into a 9- or 10-inch round fluted tart pan. Freeze for at least 30 minutes before baking.

Preheat the oven to 375°F.

Bake the tart shell until golden, about 15 minutes. Decrease the oven temperature to 325°F.

Stir together the mascarpone, sugar, eggs, lime zest and juice, and vanilla in a medium bowl until thoroughly combined. Lightly whip the cream in a separate bowl, then fold into the mascarpone mixture. Pour into the prebaked tart shell and bake until the custard is just set, 20 to 25 minutes. Cool on a rack. Chill thoroughly.

To caramelize the top, pour a thin layer of sugar evenly over the top of the tart to cover. Gently spread with an offset spatula, being careful not to upset the filling. Heat the sugar using a kitchen torch, until caramelized all over.

lemon almond cake

The addition of ground almonds gives lemony pound cake a lovely, sandy texture and makes it lighter overall. Top with a spoonful of crème fraîche and ripe blackberries for a heartier dessert; then toast leftover slices in a black cast-iron skillet and smear with marmalade-butter for a decadent breakfast treat the following day.

The cake can be made in either a Bundt pan, as pictured, or in a loaf pan. For the latter, throw a small handful of granulated sugar on top before baking to give it a crackly effect. Drizzle with a lemon glaze and lemon zest or simply dust with confectioners' sugar to serve.

MAKES 1 CAKE, SERVING 8 TO 10

½ cup blanched whole almonds

1 cup plus 2 tablespoons sugar

1 ¼ cups flour

1 ½ teaspoons baking powder

¼ teaspoon salt

1 cup (2 sticks) butter,
   at room temperature

Finely grated zest of 1 lemon

¼ cup fresh lemon juice

4 eggs

1 vanilla bean, split lengthwise

Preheat the oven to 350°F. Lightly grease a small Bundt pan or a 5- by 9-inch loaf pan; dust with flour, shaking out the excess.

Grind the almonds with 2 tablespoons of the sugar until fairly fine but with some texture. Sift the flour, baking powder, and salt into a medium bowl; stir in the ground almonds and set aside.

Using a stand mixer, beat the remaining 1 cup sugar, butter, and zest until light and fluffy. Beat in the lemon juice. Add the eggs, one at a time, beating well after each addition. Using the tip of a small knife, scrape the seeds of the vanilla pod into the mixture; beat until combined. Add the flour mixture, beating just until blended.

Spread the batter evenly in the prepared pan and bake until a cake tester inserted in the center comes out clean, about 50 minutes. Transfer the cake to a rack and cool in the pan for 15 minutes. Carefully slide a small knife around the edges of the cake to loosen. Invert the cake onto a rack, and invert again onto a second rack. Cool completely.

Do you know the land where the lemon-trees flower?

–Goethe

*Everything is blooming most recklessly; if it were voices instead of colors,
there would be an unbelievable shrieking into the heart of the night.*

−Rainer Maria Rilke, *Letters of Rainer Maria Rilke, 1892-1910*

2
still life
with berries

Eternal Spring

b e r r i e s

Beautiful, delicate berries . . . these little gumdrops of flavor are often the first sign of spring, along with ruby stalks of rhubarb and little birds singing out our window at dawn. Fragrant, thimble-like raspberries and petite, woodland strawberries—known as *fraises des bois* in France—may be the first to show up after months of everything feeling barren, nature's charm after the winter rains. Only later the curtain widens to include heart-shaped strawberries, antioxidant-rich blueberries, and a whole plethora of blackberry types to choose from, the latter improving in flavor as the days heat up and often found into early fall. Grape-like gooseberries, among other smaller bush fruits, remind me of the colder places in the world, where they are made into savory sauces, jams, crumbles, and fools; not to be confused with the cape gooseberry, a trade winds fruit characterized by its small, orange fruit and papery, outer skin, more similar to a tomato. And what about the earthy, dark purple huckleberry that grows wild from here to Montana? Known to both Native Americans and bears, and to friends of mine who seek them out in the hills each year, they make a beautiful sauce for wild salmon or roast meats, as well are lovely served with late harvest fruit, like pears. I have a thing for currants—red, white, and black, "smiling with a knowing air" as Emile Zola put it in *The Belly of Paris*. Pair these rarified beauties with raspberries, "scorched by the hot caresses of the voluptuous sun," to enhance a rhubarb sorbet, or cook with a little sugar and swirl through lightly whipped cream to dress up layers of crisp meringue. Like other berries, use currants fresh or cooked to add a swift but natural tartness to any dish.

rhubarb sorbet with strawberries in syrup

Rhubarb makes a voluptuous and smooth sorbet. Enhance its bright flavor by adding a handful of raspberries or red currants to the mix, and serve atop sweet, ripe strawberries doused with a little of the poaching syrup and eau de vie, a clear, colorless fruit brandy. Alcohol added to the sorbet base helps it retain a softer texture, but is not paramount. Serve with almond tuiles or meringues.

SERVES 4 TO 6

Scant 1 cup sugar

1½ cups water

2 (½-inch) pieces orange peel

½ cinnamon stick

1 star anise

1 pound fresh rhubarb,
  leaves discarded,
  sliced into ¼-inch pieces

½ cup raspberries or
  red currants (optional)

2 tablespoons vodka or
  fruit eau de vie, plus more
  for serving (optional)

2 cups ripe strawberries,
  for serving

Combine the sugar, water, orange peel, and spices in a medium pot. Bring slowly to a boil, stirring until the sugar is dissolved. Add the rhubarb; simmer for 5 minutes, or until the rhubarb is tender and just beginning to fall apart. Remove from the heat, cover, and let steep for 30 minutes.

Drain the rhubarb, reserving the cooking syrup and discarding the orange peel and spices. Simmer the syrup again until slightly reduced; reserve about ⅓ cup. Puree the rhubarb with the remaining syrup (about 1 cup) and the raspberries, if using, until smooth. Strain through a sieve. Taste for sweetness, adding a touch more sugar to taste as needed. Stir in the vodka, if using. Chill thoroughly.

A couple of hours before serving, churn the rhubarb puree in an ice cream maker, then freeze until the sorbet is just hard enough to hold its shape but still soft and easily scooped.

To serve, quarter or halve the strawberries, depending on their size, and divide among bowls. Drizzle each with a little reserved chilled syrup and a splash more eau de vie. Top with a scoop or two of the rhubarb sorbet and serve.

Summer's garden bed on the plate, a rather fine lunch or supper staged in the orchard. Enjoy with a glass of rosé or sparkling wine and, if by oneself, a good book.

strawberry, nasturtium, and cucumber salad

SERVES 4

Vinaigrette

1 shallot, finely chopped

1½ tablespoons champagne vinegar or white balsamic vinegar

Pinch sugar

2 strawberries

2 teaspoons finely chopped tarragon or basil

¼ cup grapeseed or sunflower oil

1 tablespoon water

Salt and freshly ground black pepper

Salad

4 cups mâche

2 cups arugula or watercress

1 seedless cucumber or 2 small Persian cucumbers, peeled, halved lengthwise, and sliced into half-moons

1 cup ripe strawberries, quartered

1 small red onion, halved, thinly sliced and pickled (see Note)

Handful just-picked nasturtium flowers

2 tablespoons sunflower seeds

Ricotta salata or other semi-aged sheep's milk cheese, for shaving

To make the vinaigrette, whisk the shallot, vinegar, and sugar in a small bowl. Mash in the strawberries and tarragon and macerate for 5 minutes. Whisk in the oil and water. Season to taste with salt and pepper.

To assemble the salad, mix the mâche and arugula in a bowl. Add the cucumber and strawberries and toss with vinaigrette to taste. Arrange on plates and scatter with the pickled onions, nasturtiums, and sunflower seeds. Shave the cheese over the tops, then finish each salad with a few twists of fresh black pepper.

NOTE: To quick-pickle the onion, blanch for 2 minutes in salted boiling water. Drain and place in a shallow bowl. Douse with a little vinegar to just cover and a pinch of sugar. Macerate until lightly pickled, 20 to 30 minutes, or longer to taste.

wild strawberry tartlets

In early spring, when the wild strawberries appeared on the path outside our cabin door, we would make these delicate tartlets, fitting for teatime under the boughs of the orange tree just across the way. Both the dough and pastry cream can be prepared ahead, making assembly that much easier and more fun. These are also quite lovely made with blackberries or sliced strawberries.

Sweet dough

½ cup (1 stick) butter,
   at room temperature

1 cup flour

¼ cup confectioners' sugar, sifted

Pinch salt

Pastry Cream

3 egg yolks

⅓ cup granulated sugar

1 tablespoon flour

1 cup whole milk

About 2 teaspoons
   orange flower or rose water

About 2 cups wild strawberries
   (or other berries)

To make the dough, beat the butter with the flour, confectioners' sugar, and salt until just combined. Press the dough evenly into 12 (3-inch) tartlet cups and freeze for about 15 minutes before baking. The dough can be made ahead, wrapped in plastic prior to forming, and refrigerated for up to 3 days, or longer in the freezer. Bring to room temperature before pressing into the tartlet molds.

To make the pastry cream, beat the yolks and granulated sugar until ribbons form. Sift in the flour and beat until combined. Heat the milk to just under a boil. Slowly add one-third of the hot milk to the egg mixture to temper. Return the combined mixture back to the pot. Cook over low heat, whisking continuously, until thickened, about 5 minutes. Strain the pastry cream into a bowl and stir in the flower water to taste. Press a piece of plastic wrap on the surface of the cream while cooling. Chill thoroughly.

Preheat the oven to 375°F.

To assemble, bake the tart shells for 5 to 7 minutes, until golden. Let cool, then gently pop the shells out of the pans and arrange on a serving tray.

Spoon the chilled pastry cream into the cooled shells. Don't do this too far ahead, as they are best eaten within an hour or so of assembling. Top with wild strawberries, leaving some with their flowers and stems for decoration.

blackberry polenta muffins

ine-grain polenta gives these muffins a tender, sandy crumb, a natural foil for juicy sweet blackberries or boysenberries. Freeze fresh berries, separated on a tray, before folding into the batter so they don't drop to the bottom while cooking. Serve warm with softened butter and a drizzle of honey.

MAKES 9 TO 12 MUFFINS

1 cup all-purpose flour

½ cup whole-wheat flour

½ cup fine polenta or
   stone-ground cornmeal

1 tablespoon baking powder

⅔ cup brown sugar

Finely grated zest of 1 orange

2 eggs

½ cup plus 2 tablespoons milk

⅓ cup safflower or
   other vegetable oil

1 cup blackberries or boysenberries

Preheat the oven to 350°F. Liberally butter or grease 9 to 12 cups of a standard muffin tin or line with paper baking cups.

Combine the flours, polenta, and baking powder in a bowl; mix well. Stir in the sugar and orange zest. Lightly whisk together the eggs, milk, and oil in a separate bowl, then stir into the flour mixture. Fold in the berries. Scoop the batter into the prepared muffin cups. Bake until golden, about 15 minutes.

Nobody in the lane, and nothing, nothing but blackberries . . .

–Sylvia Plath, from "Blackberrying"

meaty steak on a bed of hearty, leafy greens is the ideal match for racy blackberries in a vinaigrette. Make after a day of picking these late-summer beauties, when they are sun-kissed and leaching their gorgeous crimson dye all over your hands.

crimson afternoon: steak with blackberries

SERVES 4 AS A MAIN DISH,
OR MORE AS PART OF A SPREAD

2 teaspoons coriander seed, toasted

2 teaspoons pink peppercorns

2 (8-ounce) New York strip steaks

Kosher salt

½ small red onion or
1 large shallot, finely diced

3 tablespoons red wine vinegar

1½ cups blackberries

⅓ cup extra virgin olive oil

2 teaspoons thyme leaves

6 to 8 opal basil leaves,
cut into chiffonade

Aged balsamic vinegar

Salt and freshly
ground black pepper

3 to 4 cups mixed leafy greens
in a range of colors and texture,
like shiso, spinach, arugula,
and Lolla Rossa

Coarsely grind the coriander and peppercorns in a mortar and pestle. Sprinkle on both sides of each steak and season with kosher salt. Let sit at room temperature for 30 minutes before grilling.

Meanwhile, fire up the outdoor grill to medium heat (or use a grill pan on the stove) and make the blackberry dressing.

Cover the onion with the wine vinegar in a medium bowl and let sit for about 5 minutes to soften the flavors. Add ½ cup of the blackberries to the onion and gently crush with a fork, dispersing the rich color and juice. Whisk in the olive oil, thyme, basil, and a touch of balsamic vinegar to finish. You may want to add a tablespoon or so of water to round out the flavors and loosen the vinaigrette. Season with salt and pepper.

Grill the steaks to desired doneness, 4 to 6 minutes per side for medium-rare, depending on thickness. Transfer to a board, loosely tent with foil, and let rest for 5 to 10 minutes. Thinly slice across the grain.

Place the salad greens on a platter or individual plates and top with the steak slices. Drizzle the dressing over the top and scatter with the remaining 1 cup blackberries.

Ratafia is a Mediterranean aperitif typically made with macerated fruit, eau de vie (a clear fruit brandy), a bit of sugar, and occasionally herbs or other flavorings. In Provence, they might fortify ratafia with white or red wine and sometimes grappa. In Spain, they make a fruit liqueur with bitter almonds. Other regions make a version with the pits of sour cherries, a cousin to Cherry Bounce, the old-fashioned cordial made in the American South. This version is made with less sugar, my preference for a drink to stimulate the palate, not undo it. Experiment with different flavors and fruits, like summer peaches with basil leaves, white wine, and brandy. Be sure to plan ahead: It takes a minimum of 4 weeks for the alcohol and fruit to do their thing (though only about 5 minutes to put it together), and it improves with age.

raspberry ratafia

MAKES 1 BOTTLE

3 cups organic raspberries, picked over

⅓ to ½ cup sugar

1 (750 ml) bottle unflavored 80-proof vodka or eau de vie

6 verbena leaves, crushed

In a 2-quart glass jar with clamp lid, combine the raspberries and sugar, stirring to gently crush some of the berries and release their juice. Pour the vodka over and add the verbena leaves, gently crushing them between your fingers as you drop them in. Stir until the sugar is dissolved. Seal the jar and leave in a warm area of the house for a minimum of 4 to 6 weeks. Give it a good shake every few days for the first week or so to help release the flavors. Strain the ratafia into a sterilized bottle and store in a dark cool place. It should keep indefinitely.

Serve the ratafia chilled and straight up with some toasted almonds as a start to a meal, or pour over ice with a splash of white wine and garnish with fresh verbena leaves for a sexy summer cocktail.

NOTE: After the fruit has macerated for a month, you can add more sugar if you prefer it sweeter. Make a simple syrup by heating ⅓ cup water with 1 cup sugar until the sugar is dissolved; add to the ratafia to taste before bottling.

...stening to Leonard Cohen and ...ing about tomorrow. About ...York hotel rooms, oranges ...d the blues.

Hazel mist drifts across the canyon, up and over the studio where we live amidst a tumble of Victorian roses and night-blooming jasmine. It's early. My children, warm and tender like just-rising bread, are spooned in the same bed; I have slipped out, to write on the porch with my cup of coffee. Tiny wild strawberries grow on the path between our homes, and all around, the first growth of new fruit arrives seemingly overnight: Apple blossoms blushing against soft virescent leaves, mulberries fattening, nubby peaches the size of peas, and the first kiss of a pomegranate orb growing out of its brilliant flower. The lemon tree continues bearing its golden fruit, Boccaccio's orange, fragrant and full, still weighted with its fiery globes. Time to make marmalade again. Pick lupine for the table, posies of fragrant lavender for the bath. We later draw and dream and play happily on the hill in the early warmth, turn the damp, moist earth to find worms and lay seed.

*Pickles and chutneys were in demand, for much cold roast beef was eaten,
and all pickles were made at home.*

—Alison Uttley, *Recipes from an Old Farmhouse*

rhubarb mustard

*T*his is not quite mustard (after the Italian fruit mostardas), nor jam, but something in between, both sweet and savory and a little spicy. It's inspired by an unexpected visit to Incanto restaurant in San Francisco—known for their house-made salumi—with my photographer, Sara Remington. As always, our discussion that night took us all over the map and back again, inevitably returning to food, and the accoutrements, like this one, on our plate. Add this hearty condiment to the lineup of a ploughman's lunch, along with Apricot Mango Chutney (page 115), as I did for my late-summer spread pictured on pages 68–69.

MAKES ABOUT 1 CUP

½ cup water

⅓ cup malt vinegar

⅔ cup sugar

1-inch piece fresh ginger, grated

Finely grated zest of 1 lime

½ teaspoon mustard seed

Pinch salt

1 pound fresh rhubarb,
  leaves discarded,
  sliced into ½-inch pieces

1 to 2 teaspoons dry mustard

Freshly cracked black pepper

Combine the water, vinegar, sugar, ginger, lime zest, mustard seed, and salt in a medium saucepot and bring to a boil over medium-high heat. Simmer for 5 minutes, until slightly syrupy. Add half the rhubarb. Cook until it the fruit breaks down and begins to thicken, about 10 minutes. Decrease the temperature to low, add the remaining rhubarb, and cook until just tender, about 5 minutes—leave it a little chunky, as it gives the finished mustard a nice texture. Stir in the dry mustard to taste and a few cracks of fresh black pepper. Let cool, then place in a jar and refrigerate. Serve tucked in a sandwich or as part of a salumi plate.

My stepmother, Elena, built her Sweet Elena's Bakery around the humble pie. This one, made with central coast olallieberries, a cross between black loganberries and youngberries, wins every time. The name olallie comes from the Chinook Indian language, their word for all blackberries. If you can't find olallieberries, use any other type of blackberry, with a handful of raspberries thrown in to bring out that distinct, bright berry flavor. Serve with a dollop of lightly sweetened whipped cream or Crème Fraîche Ice Cream (page 150).

olallieberry pie

MAKES ONE 9-INCH
DOUBLE-CRUST PIE

Dough
2 ½ cups flour

Pinch salt

1 cup (2 sticks) chilled butter,
cut into ½-inch cubes

⅓ to ½ cup ice-cold water

Filling
4 to 5 heaping cups olallieberries

2 tablespoons cornstarch

½ to ⅔ cup sugar

Finely grated zest of ½ lemon
(about 1 teaspoon)

Pure vanilla extract (optional)

2 tablespoons cream or
1 beaten egg white, for brushing

Sanding sugar (optional)

To make the dough, place the flour and salt in the bowl of a food processor. Add the butter and pulse until it resembles coarse meal. Sprinkle with a tablespoon of cold water and pulse, adding more water a little at a time, until the dough just comes together.

Transfer the dough to a clean work surface, and, using your fingertips, work in any loose flour, gently forming the dough into a ball. Divide in half, pat into 2 disks, and wrap in plastic wrap. Chill for at least 30 minutes before rolling out.

To make the filling, in a medium bowl, combine the olallieberries, cornstarch, sugar to taste, lemon zest, and vanilla. Gently mix to coat and then let stand for 10 minutes.

Preheat the oven to 375°F.

On a lightly floured board, roll out one disk of dough into a 12-inch circle. Fit into a 9-inch pie pan, trimming any ends hanging over the side. Roll out the second disk to about the same size. For a lattice top, cut the round into ½-inch-wide strips using a fluted cutting wheel or a sharp knife, or leave whole to use as is.

Pour the berry filling into the pie shell, using a rubber spatula to scrape in all of the juices. Assemble the strips over the filling, alternating them to create the lattice pattern, or cover with the full crust. (If using the full crust, cut a few slits at the center to release some of the heat as it bakes.) Trim the top crust to size, and then pinch the edge with the bottom crust to seal.

Lightly brush the crust with a little cream or beaten egg white to help with browning; sprinkle with sanding sugar, if desired. Bake for 25 minutes, then decrease the heat to 350°F. Bake for 25 to 30 minutes more, until the crust is golden and the filling is bubbling in the center. Cool on a wire rack for at least 2 hours before serving.

Rose is a rose is a rose is a rose.

—Gertrude Stein

raspberry rhubarb rose petal jam

One of my favorite spring-summer fruit combinations is raspberries and rhubarb, set apart by a whiff of heady rose in the background—an ethereal synthesis of flavors to tease the palate for months to come. Spread this jam on thick slices of brioche toast on Sunday morning, or layer between slices of Lemon Almond Cake (page 38) with softly whipped cream, or simply spoon over vanilla ice cream scattered with more rose petals to garnish.

MAKES ABOUT TWO 8-OUNCE JARS

2 cups organic raspberries

1 pound rhubarb (about 3 stalks), leaves discarded, sliced ¼ inch thick

Scant 2 cups sugar

Handful (about 12) unsprayed rose petals

2 teaspoons rose water

Pick through and remove any funky raspberries or remaining stems, but do not wash the berries. Place in a preserving pot with the rhubarb and sprinkle with about ¼ cup water, just enough to very lightly moisten. Cover with the sugar and rose petals and let stand for an hour or so to macerate.

Bring to a gentle simmer over medium-low heat and cook, stirring on occasion, until the sugar is dissolved and the rhubarb begins to soften, about 10 minutes. Raise the temperature a smidge and cook rapidly, stirring on occasion and making sure it doesn't burn, until the ingredients meld—the roses will disintegrate—and you reach the desired set, 15 to 20 minutes more. Test the set by placing a small spoonful of warm jam on a chilled plate—it should slightly cling to the plate as you tip it; alternatively, run your finger through it after 1 minute, if it wrinkles, the jam is set.

Off the heat, skim any scum that sometimes accumulates around the edge of the pot and discard. Stir in the rose water. Ladle the jam into warm, sterilized jars and seal. Store in a cool, dark place for up to 1 year, or longer in the refrigerator.

gooseberry
yellow
plum fool

Musky in flavor with a lemony scent, gooseberries make a delicious compote and fool, solo or paired with other fruits, like plums. They are intoxicating when combined with elderflower, their spirituous soul mate. Swirl this compote into softly whipped cream blended with thick, creamy Greek yogurt for an enchanting fool's fool, a lighter twist on the classic British dessert. Or enjoy the compote by itself on crepes or pancakes.

SERVES 4 TO 6

1 cup gooseberries

6 to 8 mirabelle or other small yellow plums, pitted and chopped

⅓ cup sugar

1 to 2 teaspoons elderflower syrup

¾ cup heavy cream

¾ cup plain Greek yogurt

Top and tail the gooseberries. Place in a small saucepan with the plums and a splash of water. Cook over low to medium heat for about 5 minutes, until the plums begin to soften and the skins of the berries burst. Add the sugar and cook 5 to 10 minutes more, stirring on occasion, until the compote begins to thicken. Stir in the elderflower syrup to taste. Transfer to a bowl and let cool thoroughly before proceeding.

Whip the cream with a tad of sugar, to taste, until soft peaks form. Gently fold the cream into the yogurt. Reserve ¼ cup of the compote to garnish, then loosely swirl the remaining into the cream-yogurt mixture, leaving it less than combined for an ethereal effect. Spoon the fool into glass bowls and top with the reserved compote.

"Country life has its advantages," he used to say. "You sit on the veranda drinking tea and your ducklings swim on the pond, and everything smells good . . . and there are gooseberries."

–Anton Chekhov, from "Gooseberries"

ploughman's lunch

Much about life in the orchard is the antithesis of urban dwelling. The enjoyment of food and a shared meal, at times, can seem no different, though it's true it doesn't have to be. Even so, I often long for the slower pace of the country, the simple meals and gatherings around the table, and the natural rhythms of orchard life, when you wake and when you go to sleep at night. A spread of cured meats, aged and fresh artisan cheeses, and a selection of fruit, along with pickles, chutneys, and some good bread, are the makings of a divine country lunch, a noteworthy picnic, or a gorgeous dinner for oneself or a crowd. This brings me back home time and again. It is how we often ate then, and still today, around my worn table with friends—impromptu and unplanned.

A simple chunk of cheese and bread are the traditional makings of a ploughman's lunch, the cold snack or meal that originated in the United Kingdom and is quite popular in pubs; and it's what I return to in spirit when putting together my version of a late-summer spread or country meal. Add a bottle of crisp white wine or hearty ale and an old-fashioned Olallieberry Pie (page 59) for dessert, and savor the pleasures and bounty of orchard living.

When putting together your own spread, look for regional and local specialties at your farmers' market, like fresh cheeses, cured salamis, pâtés, and even preserves, then supplement with a few imported favorites. Consider history, the Italians pairing cured ham with melon and figs or late-summer tomatoes with mozzarella, for inspiration. Choose a spot to enjoy it, whether in the orchard or on a rooftop or in a courtyard in the city. Arrange food on colorful platters and boards, and lay all of it out on a beautiful cloth, or simply on the table under the boughs of a shade tree. Relish what is in season, what can be purchased nearby, and what takes little time to prepare. The charm comes, of course, with what you've made yourself earlier on, the pickles and preserves, like my Rhubarb Mustard (page 58) or Apricot Mango Chutney (page 115), not to mention a bounty of just-picked fresh fruit and good friends added to the fray.

I am convinced that an inspired meal along the lines of country life and a ploughman's lunch will prove to be far more satisfying and rich then something fussy or labored over, and more remarkable and striking than even the best restaurant meal.

* *The Ploughman's Lunch* is also the title of a 1985 screenplay by Ian McEwan, where it is referred to as a "completely successful fabrication of the past."

bulgur wheat salad with blueberries and preserved lemon

This beautiful combination of flavors and textures, all arriving to market around the same time, makes the perfect potluck dish. Summer's rewards on the plate, perhaps? I say, add and take away ingredients at your leisure, but be sure to make it nonetheless. Bulgur wheat, a precooked whole grain with a pleasant nutty flavor, is used in tabbouleh—it is not the same as cracked wheat, as is often suggested. Look for it at Middle Eastern stores and larger natural food markets. Quinoa or couscous would be nice substitutes if you can't find it.

SERVES 4 TO 6

1 cup bulgur wheat

Salt

1 scant cup boiling water
  or vegetable broth

½ small red onion, finely chopped

Fresh corn kernels from 1 cob

2 Persian cucumbers or
  1 English cucumber, diced

1 cup fresh blueberries

¼ cup dried blueberries, softened
  in hot water for 5 minutes

⅓ cup pine nuts, lightly toasted

1 bunch parsley or cilantro, chopped

Handful mint leaves, cut into
  chiffonade or left whole

3 to 4 tablespoons fresh lemon juice

2 pieces Preserved Lemons (page 22),
  skin only, finely chopped,
  plus slices for serving

3 tablespoons extra virgin olive oil

Freshly ground black pepper

Place the bulgur wheat in a medium bowl with a pinch of salt. Pour the boiling water over, stir, and cover; let sit for 15 to 20 minutes. Drain or squeeze out any excess water; fluff with a fork.

Meanwhile, combine the onion, corn, cucumbers, fresh and dried blueberries, pine nuts, and herbs in a separate larger bowl. Stir in the cooked bulgur, lemon juice to taste, preserved lemon, and olive oil. Season with salt and pepper. Add more lemon juice or preserved lemon to taste. Serve with thin slices of preserved lemon on the side.

Wet dew kissing the leaves like brilliant
sunshine and its shadows dancing across the skin
on a warm afternoon

Inspired by a book of summer recipes from Italy, this savory fruit risotto is surprisingly delicious, not at all cloying as one might suspect. The blueberries impart a pleasant tannic quality, as in wine-like, staining the risotto a rich violet. Rice is traditional, but this is also delicious made with farro, an ancient wheat grain popular in Italy; it has a nutty taste and is similar to, but not quite the same as, American spelt. Look for farro that is semi-pearled. In early fall, make this risotto with wild huckleberries, red wine, and a tuft of sautéed chanterelles on top.

blueberry lemon thyme risotto

SERVES 4

1 tablespoon olive oil

1 tablespoon butter

1 small white onion

1¼ cups arborio rice or farro

2 to 3 teaspoons lemon thyme leaves, plus more for garnish

Salt

1 cup white wine

1¼ cups blueberries, plus more for garnish

4 cups light chicken or vegetable stock or water, kept at a simmer

⅓ cup crème fraîche

Finely grated zest of 1 lemon

Freshly cracked black pepper

Grana Padano cheese, for grating

Heat the olive oil and butter in a medium skillet. Stir in the onion and sauté until softened, about 5 minutes. Stir in the rice, thyme, and a pinch of salt and cook for 1 minute, then add the wine and half the blueberries. Cook until the wine is almost evaporated.

Gradually add ½ cup simmering stock, stirring until the stock is fully incorporated. Repeat with the remaining stock, ½ cup at a time, cooking until the rice is al dente, about 30 minutes overall. Add the crème fraîche and lemon zest towards the end, stirring vigorously until incorporated and the rice is creamy. Stir in the remaining blueberries and cook for 1 minute. Season with more salt and freshly cracked black pepper. Divide the risotto among 4 bowls and grate cheese over each serving. Garnish each with a few berries, if desired, and a bit more thyme to finish.

Wild salmon and earthy huckleberries make good bedfellows; both come in season in late summer/early fall and are native to the Americas. Seek out a patch of the bluish-black berries to gather for yourself if possible, as it's rare to find them in stores and if you do they are quite expensive. A tuft of lightly seasoned Bloomsdale spinach or mâche pairs beautifully with the rich salmon and sauce.

herb-roasted salmon with wild huckleberry sauce

SERVES 4

4 (6-ounce) wild salmon fillets

Salt and freshly ground black pepper

1 tablespoon olive oil, plus more for brushing

2 tablespoons mixed chopped herbs, such as parsley, thyme, and tarragon

Scant 1 tablespoon butter

1 medium shallot, finely chopped

¼ cup dry white wine or vegetable stock

1 cup huckleberries

1 teaspoon honey

1 teaspoon finely grated lemon zest

1 teaspoon chopped tarragon or thyme

Splash balsamic vinegar

Preheat the oven to 375°F.

Season the salmon fillets liberally on both sides with salt and pepper. Over medium heat, heat the olive oil in an ovenproof sauté pan large enough to hold all the fillets, or use two smaller pans. Add the salmon, skin side down, and cook for 2 to 3 minutes, until lightly browned on the bottom. Brush the tops with a little more oil, sprinkle with the herbs, and place the pan in the preheated oven. Roast until the fish is just opaque in the center, about 12 minutes depending on the thickness and size of fillets.

Meanwhile, heat the butter in a skillet over medium heat. Add the shallot and sauté until soft, 2 to 3 minutes. Stir in the wine and huckleberries and simmer until slightly thick and saucy, about 5 minutes. Stir in the honey, lemon zest, tarragon, and vinegar. Cook for 1 minute more. Season to taste with salt and pepper. Spoon the warm sauce over the salmon and serve.

almond meringue with rose cream and red currants

Sweet, crackly meringue provides a decadent stage for luscious folds of scented cream and berries in this gorgeous dessert. I especially love tart red currants paired with rose and almond, a heavenly combination that reminds me of the extravagant, far-flung flavors of Tunisia, where I once spent a month. White currants tend to be a little sweeter than red and also make a nice garnish as shown. Dress the whole affair with rose petals or rose geranium flowers.

SERVES 8 TO 10

Meringue

⅓ cup whole almonds

1 cup plus 2 tablespoons sugar

5 egg whites

Pinch salt

1 teaspoon white vinegar

2 teaspoons orange flower or rose water

Red Currant Sauce

1½ cups red (and/or white) currants, plus more for garnish

3 to 4 tablespoons sugar

Drop vanilla extract or orange flower water

Rose Cream

1 cup heavy cream

3 tablespoons sugar or warmed honey

2 teaspoons rose water, or more to taste

Unsprayed rose petals, for garnish

Confectioners' sugar, for dusting

Preheat the oven to 275°F. Draw two 8-inch circles on parchment paper with a pencil and lightly grease the areas with butter or a neutral oil, like canola. Place on a large baking sheet.

To make the meringue, coarsely grind the almonds with 2 tablespoons of the sugar in a food processor. In a stand mixer using a whisk attachment, beat the egg whites with the salt until frothy. Add a couple tablespoons of sugar and beat until the whites begin to peak. Gradually add more sugar, beating until the whites are glossy and almost tripled in volume but not stiff or lumpy. Beat in the vinegar and flower water. Dust the sugared almonds over the top and quickly fold in by hand to incorporate.

Loosely spread the meringue onto the marked parchment, allowing it to loop and swirl. Place the baking sheet on the middle rack of the oven, and immediately reduce the temperature to 250°F. Bake for 1 to 1½ hours, until the meringues are fairly set and no longer tacky to the touch. During baking, lower the temperature even more as necessary to maintain an even heat and avoid excessive browning, and occasionally rotate the baking sheet so the meringues bake evenly throughout. The meringues should be fairly white to light tan.

Cool the meringues on the baking sheet in the oven with the door slightly ajar for a few hours, up to overnight. Meringues crisp up as they cool. Wrap tightly in plastic wrap and keep in a cool place for up to 3 days, or freeze for longer storage.

To make the currant sauce, stem the currants and place in a saucepot with sugar to taste. Bring to a simmer and cook until the berries burst and the mixture becomes saucy, about 5 minutes. Stir in the vanilla and transfer to a small bowl. Let cool before using.

To make the rose cream, whip the cream with the sugar until soft peaks form. Beat in the rose water, adding more to taste. Spread the cream loosely on top of the bottom meringue. Drizzle half of the cooled red currant sauce over the cream, stirring some of it through the cream to create a swirled effect. Top with the other meringue, spreading with more cream and sauce. Garnish with whole currants and rose petals and dust lightly with confectioners' sugar. It's best if assembled within a couple of hours of serving.

3

plum
gorgeous

Remembered Mornings, and Summer Afternoons

stone fruit

Fleshy, aromatic peaches and smooth-skinned nectarines, juicy plums, delicate apricots, and sweet, vibrant cherries are at the heart of summertime goodness and what I look forward to most come June, when they first begin to appear. I relish my first taste of a tangy nectarine to remind me of a picnic in Paris by the river long ago, or a bite of ambrosial peach, its honeyed juice running down my chin when a child. Is there anything more adorable than our own children dripping in sweet plum juice in the heat of July? I can see my own now, half-naked and rambling through the orchard to climb the groaning plum tree that hovered over our orchard home, eating as much in one sitting as they managed to gather for the rustic hand pies we would make together later that day or for the lavender-scented jam that I would eventually pot and they would have for breakfast.

Rarely do you see the farmers' markets as packed as when these celebrated fruits are in—cherries being the harbinger of all drupes to follow. We jostle for tastes from the vendor's sample box to help us choose between the many unusual varieties now available, like the scarlet striped Indian Blood peach, or the ruby-fleshed Elephant Heart (or blood) plum. Part of the fun is trying to capture the essence of a particular fruit, whether it be preserved in a jar to savor later, or encased in a buttery crust and baked, or perhaps mellowed in lightly sweetened syrups with rose or verbena, or simply preserved in alcohol and wine as is done in France and Italy.

plum blackberry sorbet

Scarlet-purple plums combined with blackberries (or black currants, if you can find them) make for a gorgeously rich sorbet with a voluptuous, almost creamy texture—perfectly satisfying after a heavy meal and sophisticated enough to serve on special occasions. Add a touch of cassis to bring out the deep berry flavor and serve with slices of fresh fruit or meringue cookies.

SERVES 4

1 pound plums, pitted and chopped
1 cup blackberries or black currants
½ cup sugar
1 tablespoon cassis
About 1 teaspoon lemon juice

Simmer the plums with the blackberries, sugar, and about ¼ cup water (more or less depending on the ripeness of the fruit) in a small saucepan over low heat until soft and pulpy, 5 to 10 minutes. Let cool slightly, then puree and press through a sieve to remove seeds and skin. You should have about 2 cups puree. Stir in the cassis and lemon juice to taste. Chill thoroughly, then churn in an ice cream maker. Freeze until hardened, about 1 hour.

Remembered mornings, light streaming through the window, wild plums falling by the cabin door, barefoot children, llamas, and sunshine. Afternoons above the fog line, blackberries for tea, lavender blossoms, roses, and pale pink peonies.

This is one of my all-time favorite desserts, capturing everything I love about cooking from the orchard—just-picked ripe fruit, along with herbs from the garden. Choose firm but ripe, deep purple plums with richly colored flesh, like Burgundy, for the best flavor, gorgeous color, and "wow" factor. Basil adds a heady note to the ice cream and is a perfect sweet-savory foil for the fruit-forward soup. Lemon verbena is a good substitute. On another occasion, try pairing the basil ice cream with poached white nectarines and raspberry sauce (page 120), served in a tall glass, a play on the classic Melba.

plum soup with basil ice cream

SERVES 4 TO 6

Plum Soup
¾ cup sugar
1 cup Pinot Noir wine
½ cup water
1 vanilla bean, split lengthwise
Grated zest of 1 lime
8 dark purple ripe plums
Cassis (optional)
Basil leaves, for garnish

Basil Ice Cream
2 cups whole milk
1 cup heavy cream
½ cup sugar
Large handful basil leaves, bruised
2 (½-inch) strips lemon peel, from an organic lemon
4 egg yolks, lightly beaten

Combine the sugar, wine, and water in a saucepot. Scrape the vanilla seeds into the pot, drop in the pod, and add the zest. Bring to a boil over medium heat; simmer for 10 to 15 minutes, until syrupy and reduced by nearly half. Chill thoroughly, and then strain, reserving the vanilla pod to flavor a jar of sugar (once dried).

Meanwhile, pit the plums and puree in a food processor. Strain the pulp through a sieve into a glass bowl.

Stir about half the strained chilled syrup into the plum puree (or just enough to achieve desired consistency and flavor). Add a drop or two of cassis, if desired. Chill thoroughly. Before serving, swirl in more wine syrup to thin, as needed. It should have body but still be somewhat loose and soupy. Reserve any remaining syrup for another use—it's delicious drizzled over slices of pound cake or ice cream.

Pour the soup into bowls or glass cups and serve each with a scoop of basil ice cream. Garnish with basil leaves.

For the ice cream, combine the milk, ½ cup of the cream, the sugar, basil, and lemon peel in a saucepot over medium heat. Bring to just under a boil, stirring to dissolve the sugar, then remove from the heat. Cover and steep for 30 minutes, or longer for a more pronounced flavor.

Remove the basil and lemon pieces. Return to the heat. Temper the eggs by stirring in one-third of the hot milk mixture, then pouring the mixture back into the pot. Cook over low heat, stirring, until the mixture coats the back of a spoon, about 5 minutes. Pour into a bowl set over ice and stir in the remaining ½ cup cream. Chill thoroughly before churning in an ice cream maker. Harden in the freezer for 1 hour before serving.

spiced plums

*D*elicious served with cheese or as part of a ploughman's lunch, these plums are also divine when grilled as an accompaniment to chicken or pork, like Lavender-Brined Pork Chops (opposite page). They can be put up in jars for longer storage and improved flavor or made the day you plan to eat them. If the plums are particularly small, don't bother halving the fruit; simply prick with a toothpick and poach whole, adding a minute or so to the cooking time. Depending on the variety of plums you use and how long you cook them, the skin may shrivel and fall off. If preparing to use for the grill, poach them the least amount of time, just enough to imbue them with flavor, and let them sit in the syrup until cool.

MAKES 1 QUART

1 cup turbinado or
  Demerara sugar

1 cup apple cider vinegar
  or malt vinegar

½ cup water

1 cinnamon stick

1 sprig rosemary

½ vanilla bean

1 bay leaf

3 allspice berries

Few grinds freshly ground
  black pepper

About 1½ pounds red plums,
  halved and pitted

Combine the sugar, vinegar, and water in a medium saucepot and bring to a low boil, stirring occasionally until the sugar dissolves. Add the cinnamon, rosemary, vanilla bean, bay leaf, allspice, and a few cracks of black pepper; boil gently for about 5 minutes. Add the plums and gently poach at a simmer for 1 minute, or a bit longer if they are large or it seems necessary. They can overcook pretty quickly—you want them cooked enough to soak up the flavors, but still firm so they don't fall apart. Transfer the plums with a slotted spoon to a sterilized quart jar. Bring the spiced syrup back to a boil and cook until thick and syrupy, about 5 minutes. Pour over plums, along with the spices. Seal and store in a cool, dark place for several weeks.

The lavender- and herb-scented brine adds a subtle floral note to these meaty chops while tenderizing them at the same time. The chops need to soak in the brine, preferably overnight, so plan ahead. Similarly, make a jar of these spiced plums ahead, then grill them alongside the pork until soft and slightly charred, a lavish pairing indeed. Figure about 1 cup of brine per chop and 3 or 4 plum halves per person.

lavender-brined pork chops with grilled spiced plums

SERVES 4 TO 6

¼ cup kosher salt

3 tablespoons sugar

1 onion, quartered

2 cloves garlic, crushed

Leaves from 2 sprigs rosemary

Leaves from 2 sprigs thyme

1 bay leaf

Few grinds fresh black pepper

Large pinch lavender flowers

4 to 6 bone-in pork chops,
8 to 10 ounces each

1 to 2 tablespoons olive oil

1 recipe Spiced Plums
(opposite page)

To make the brine, mix the salt and sugar with 2 cups of warm to hot water, stirring until dissolved. Add the onion, garlic, rosemary, thyme, bay leaf, black pepper, and lavender flowers, plus 6 to 8 cups cold water, or enough to cover the pork chops. Submerge the chops in the brine, cover, and refrigerate overnight.

Remove the chops from the brine; discard the brine. Pat the chops dry and let them sit out for 30 minutes to come to room temperature.

Prepare an outdoor grill to medium, or heat a large grill pan over medium heat. Brush the pork chops lightly with the oil and place on the grill. Cook for 7 to 10 minutes, depending on thickness, until nicely charred on one side, occasionally rotating them so they cook evenly. Turn them over and cook for about 5 minutes more, rotating them again, until medium-rare to medium.

Once you turn the pork, add the plums to the grill. Cook, turning them over every so often and basting them with some of the spiced syrup (reducing it a little first), until tender and slightly charred. Arrange the chops on a platter, surround with the grilled plums, and drizzle with some of the syrup.

cherry clafoutis

Sweet black cherries baked in custard is a specialty of the Limousin region of France; it's a popular no-fuss dessert served warm or cold, dusted with a little sugar. Traditionally the cherries are left whole, so that the pits imbue a little of their almond flavor. This is how I've always done it too, though you can surely pit them (and my daughter thinks I should); in fact most people do. Try making the clafoutis with other stone fruit like plums and peaches or, in the fall, fresh figs or dried prunes soaked first in brandy for a twist.

SERVES 6 TO 8

4 cups sweet cherries

½ cup turbinado or Demerara sugar

1 to 2 tablespoons kirsch

6 eggs

1 cup whole milk

⅔ cup crème fraîche

2 teaspoons pure vanilla extract

6 tablespoons flour

Pinch salt

⅓ cup sliced almonds, lightly toasted

Confectioners' sugar (optional)

Wash and stem the cherries and pit if you prefer; pat dry. In a bowl, toss the cherries with 2 tablespoons of the sugar and the kirsch, more or less as you like to taste. Set aside at room temperature for at least 20 minutes, allowing the flavors to meld.

Preheat the oven to 400°F.

Generously butter a 9-inch cast-iron skillet or earthenware dish. Scatter the cherries in the bottom of the dish.

Combine the remaining 6 tablespoons sugar, the eggs, milk, crème fraîche, vanilla, flour, and salt in a blender. Blend to combine thoroughly; strain if necessary to remove any lumps of flour, then whisk back in by hand.

Pour the custard over the cherries. Bake the clafoutis for 35 to 40 minutes, until puffy and golden and just set in the middle. Sprinkle with the toasted almonds and dust with confectioners' sugar, if you like, before serving.

A lighter, more summery twist on the typical duck, cherries tango with a touch of cinnamon and spice—just right for a shared meal on the terrace with friends. The cherry salsa also pairs well with chicken and pork. Or stir it through couscous and add a drizzle of olive oil for an effortless grain and fruit salad.

honey-glazed duck breasts with cherry salsa

Serves 3 or 4 as a starter course

2 (10- to 12-ounce) boneless duck breasts, preferably Muscovy

1 to 2 teaspoons freshly ground coriander seed

Salt and freshly ground black pepper

¼ cup honey

Pinch cinnamon

Salsa
½ pound fresh cherries, halved, pitted, and some of them quartered

½ red onion or 1 large shallot, finely chopped

¼ cup almonds, lightly toasted and coarsely chopped

1 jalapeño pepper, seeded and minced

Juice of 1 lime

⅓ bunch cilantro, leaves coarsely chopped

Few mint leaves, cut into chiffonade

While they are still cold, score the skin side of the duck breasts—a few slits or crosshatches about ½ inch wide, almost down to the meat. Season with the coriander, salt, and pepper. Leave at room temperature, loosely covered, for 30 minutes before cooking.

Gently warm the honey with a pinch of cinnamon. Reserve for basting the duck and adding to the salsa.

Meanwhile, make the salsa. Combine the cherries, onion, almonds, jalapeño to taste (better to add less to start), and about 1 tablespoon honey in a bowl. Stir in the lime juice, cilantro, and mint. Season to taste with salt and pepper.

Heat a nonstick skillet over medium-high heat. Add the duck breasts, skin side down, and then immediately decrease the heat to medium-low. Cook until the fat is rendered (pouring it off into a jar as you go) and the skin turns a deep golden color, about 10 minutes. While cooking, brush the breasts with a little warmed honey. Turn the breasts over and cook to medium-rare (130°F), a few minutes more depending on thickness. Transfer to a cutting board, cover loosely with foil, and let rest for 5 minutes.

Slice the breasts on the diagonal, arranging slices on plates or a large platter. Top with the salsa, drizzle with any remaining honey, and serve.

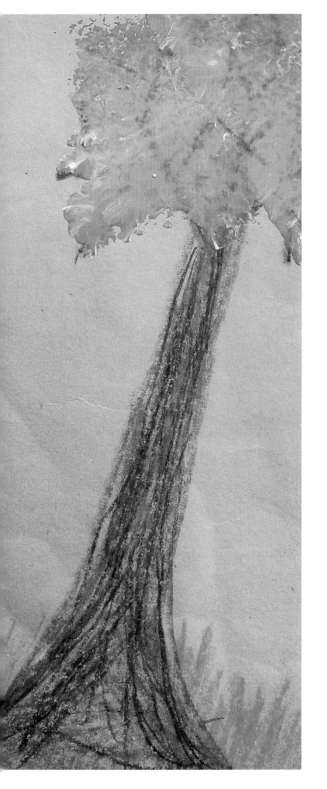

Late-harvest
fog drifting
through the orchard,
heat subsiding
plums
falling
away

Summer in the orchard had a particular mood and feel to it: warm and grassy, the sweet aroma of chamomile, lavender, and honey-scented apricots lingering in the air. Long-lasting mornings and longer evenings with generous gatherings around the table. The little ones lost to teddy bear teas and fanciful games in the heat of the day, to horses and goats and theatrical debuts. Outings to the pool at the top of the hill in the late afternoon, picnics made up almost entirely of orchard fruit. Imagine glistening jars of sun-ripened tomatoes and downy peaches on the shelf; an abundance of lemons for lemonade, bunches of sweet basil and plump figs on the table, and gorgeous rosy colored rhubarb stalks reaching for the sky just out our cabin door. For me, it was not summer without the sticky, purple stain of wild plums on my fingers, a large pot of jam bubbling on the stove, the drone of cicadas at nightfall, my kids idling under the golden globes of a loquat tree way past their bedtime.

wild plum lavender jam

What I especially love about this jam is that it takes little or no care at the start of the process, and when faced with a glut of wild plums in the heat of summer—wherever there are trees, practically—it's an easy and fast way to deal with them right off, before they begin to ferment. You will need a large sieve for straining the fruit after it cooks. How much jam you end up with changes according to the amount of fruit you start with.

Wild plums, rinsed and stemmed
Sugar
Lavender flowers
Fresh lemon juice (optional)

Wild plums seem to grow just about everywhere I've lived, whether in the city or in the orchard, and currently right out my kitchen door, hovering over the fence at my neighbors next to their bees. Cherry in size, varied in flavor and color—from red to purple to golden yellow—they are the perfect jam fruit, refusing to be pitted prior to cooking and making for a divine, clear and delicious, ethereal-tasting preserve.

In a very large pot, place as many plums as the pot can manage with ½ inch (at most) of water at the bottom. Cook over low to medium heat, stirring on occasion, until the fruit is very soft and pulpy, about 45 minutes. Cool slightly, and then strain the mixture in a large cone sieve placed over a second pot, pressing hard on the solids to extract the pulp and juices. Discard the remaining solids and pits.

Measure the pulp. For every cup, you will want to add a scant ¾ cup sugar, perhaps a little less or more depending on how sweet you like your jam. You can start with less, and add more as desired later. Or simply eyeball it with as much sugar as you think it will need, a method my sister Sara uses quite regularly with great success. Add a small handful of lavender flowers. (Simply pick unsprayed lavender stems and leave them out in the sun for a few days, then pull off the flowers when dried. Fresh lavender flowers will work too, but dried seems to offer more concentrated flavor.)

Once you've added the sugar and lavender, bring the mixture to a simmer over low to medium heat, gently stirring to dissolve the sugar. When dissolved, raise the temperature a smidge, then cook at a fairly rapid simmer, stirring on occasion, for 30 to 40 minutes, until desired setting point is reached. To check the set, place a spoonful on a cold plate and let sit for 1 minute. Then run your finger through it; it should wrinkle and feel firm.

More often than not, I allow the jam pot to sit on the stove for a day (or longer), after it has cooked once, allowing the flavors to develop. Then I add more sugar to taste, or a squeeze of lemon juice, if needed, and cook again. At this point, watch it more closely so it doesn't burn—or turn a deep, rosy amber color (at which point you will have more of a plum butter—yummy too). Pot the jam in sterilized jars, top with hot lids and bands, and turn the jars over for 1 hour to help complete the seal. Store in a dark cupboard for up to a year, or longer in the refrigerator.

② Spiced Plums

③ — Plums for Jam

① — Rhubarb Mustard

epitaph for love

In his book Epitaph for a Peach, *third-generation Japanese-American farmer David Mas Masumoto recounts the struggles and joys of his year-long attempt to keep alive the Sun Crest peach, a fragile, older variety with red-blushed skin. It grows in California's San Joaquin Valley, but is nearly lost to newer types lauded by growers today. As I stumbled upon a box of Masumoto's fragile peaches at my local grocer recently, I recall my own joy in sharing in his family's annual harvest of the yellow-fleshed, late-ripening Elberta, another heirloom peach, a few years ago. That day, I basked in the intoxicating aroma of ripe fruit that permeated the sun-drenched orchard, and enjoyed the simple breakfast of French toast with sliced peaches that was served by his wife and children on paper plates to the many who gathered to help with the harvest—the poets, painters, musicians, chefs, neighbors, and lovers of lore. Masumoto's lyrical descriptions of daily life on his family's farm and his quest to preserve not only his heritage but also a peach with true flavor came to life that day, a delicious reflection on the choices we make—not for money so much as for love.*

fresh peach gelato

Make this gelato in late summer when the peaches are at their peak, their honey fragrance permeating the house. Serve on cones for the kids, or with just-picked blackberries doused with a little Moscato wine or orange essence for a more grown-up dessert.

Gelato is best eaten within a couple hours of being churned and frozen. Start this a day ahead, as the base needs to ripen, preferably overnight.

MAKES ABOUT 1 QUART

1½ cups whole milk

¾ cup heavy cream

⅔ to 1 cup vanilla sugar

1½ tablespoons cornstarch

Small pinch salt

2 tablespoons orange blossom honey

3 ripe large peaches

Orange flower water or Moscato wine

Combine the milk and ½ cup of the cream in a medium saucepot. Whisk ½ cup of the sugar with the cornstarch and salt until blended, then whisk it into the milk mixture along with the honey. Bring to a boil over medium heat. Boil for 2 to 3 minutes, stirring on occasion, until the milk begins to thicken. Pour into a bowl set over ice, add the remaining ¼ cup cream, and whisk to cool. Chill overnight.

Meanwhile, remove the skin of the peaches: Cut an X into the stem end of each, drop in a pot of boiling water for 30 to 45 seconds, then dunk in ice water for just as long. Peel and pit the peaches, and mash in a bowl with a fork (don't puree), leaving them a little chunky. You should have about 1½ cups pulp. Stir in the remaining sugar (up to ½ cup) and the orange flower water to taste. (A little goes a long way, especially the orange flower essence; about 2 tablespoons seems to work well.) Macerate for 1 hour, or longer.

Whisk together the milk base and the fruit mixture. Churn in an ice cream or gelato machine. Freeze for 1 to 2 hours before serving.

NOTE: Occasionally, peaches need a little coaxing to ripen; if so, you can first poach them in a little bit of wine syrup, which also tastes great and can help keep the gelato softer longer. Strain before mashing, proceeding from there (adding less sugar and omitting additional wine).

Some of my favorite summer ingredients on one plate, more than suitable for a late-afternoon lunch with a glass of dry rosé and gypsy music playing in the background, a red dress blowing in the wind behind. My ode to Spain, memories from before and the ones not yet made. Choose a quality, cured ham, like serrano (literally "mountain ham") or Niman Ranch's Jambon Royale, dry cured and smoked (pictured), along with salty Spanish Marcona almonds to pair with the tangy, sweet nectarines and peppery watermelon radishes.

spanish dancer: nectarine salad with haricots verts and cured ham

Blanch the haricots verts in boiling salted water until tender to the bite, 2 to 3 minutes. Drain and rinse under cool water, then spread out on a plate or sheet pan to cool.

Whisk together the shallot, olive oil, and vinegars; add the herbs and season with salt and pepper. Whisk in 1 tablespoon of water and a pinch of sugar, if needed, to soften the vinaigrette.

Place the beans in a bowl with the watercress, nectarines, and radishes; gently toss with the vinaigrette. Arrange the salad on plates, tucking a couple slices of ham into each. Scatter with the almonds.

SERVES 3 OR 4

½ pound haricots verts

1 small shallot, finely chopped

¼ cup extra virgin olive oil

1 tablespoon sherry vinegar

2 teaspoons champagne vinegar or rice wine vinegar

Few leaves each of basil and mint, finely slivered

Salt and freshly ground black pepper

Pinch sugar (optional)

1 bunch watercress, rinsed and trimmed

2 to 3 nectarines, pitted and sliced into wedges

2 watermelon radishes, halved and thinly sliced

Several thin slices cured ham

¼ cup Marcona almonds

blenheim
apricot
preserves
(my favorite jam)

*B*lenheim apricots make the best preserves and jam and are highly sought after during their very short season. I like to flavor mine with a vanilla bean, or dried lavender flowers from the garden, which add a lovely floral note to the honeyed apricots. The trick with this recipe is to not overcook the preserves so they remain golden and clear with whole pieces of fruit. Swirl some jam into a bowl of plain thick yogurt for a celestial breakfast or light dessert, or use as a topping for ice cream or as the base for a Rustic Fruit Galette (page 112) or simply to make a jam tart.

MAKES ABOUT FOUR 8-OUNCE JARS

3 pounds Blenheim apricots, halved and quartered (6 pits reserved)

⅓ cup water

1 vanilla bean, split, or large pinch dried lavender flowers

3 cups sugar

Fresh lemon juice (optional)

Combine the apricots and water in a jam pot. Scrape in the vanilla seeds and drop in the pod (or add a large pinch lavender flowers). Cover with the sugar and set aside overnight. Crack open the reserved apricot pits, using a hammer or nutcracker, to get at the small kernel inside each. Drop the kernels into a small saucepan of water and soak overnight as well.

The next morning, bring the apricot mixture to a simmer over low heat, stirring occasionally until the sugar dissolves. Raise the heat to medium and cook for about 20 minutes, until the fruit is soft and begins to break down. Meanwhile, boil the apricot kernels separately for 5 minutes, and then add to the apricots. Add a squeeze or two of lemon juice, to taste, if needed for balance. Raise the heat a smidge and boil the jam, stirring on occasion, for 20 to 25 minutes more, until the setting point is reached. Remove any scum from the surface as it cooks.

Pot the jam into sterilized jars and top with hot lids and bands. Turn the jars over for an hour to help complete the seal. Store in a dark cupboard for up to 1 year, or longer in the refrigerator.

The Blenheim is an older, smaller variety of apricot with freckled, golden blush skin; it appears in late June for just a couple of weeks. Worth seeking out, it offers pure old-fashioned apricot flavor, best for preserves, drying, and eating out of hand. At one time, Blenheim trees grew all over California and were prized for their delicate flavor, perfectly captured when sun-dried. Unfortunately, they have slowly given way to less flavorful varieties that are cheaper to grow and better for shipping, or as one local farmer told me, to a growing Turkish trade.

Gorgeously summer, in every way. I adore this salad for everything it is–simple, elegant, and full of bright flavors, and for everything it's not–fancy, fussy, and difficult to put together. Burrata, a buttery soft, fresh cheese akin to mozzarella but filled with cream, pairs beautifully with both fruits–yes, tomato is in fact a fruit. Look for an old-fashioned peach, like Elberta, a deep yellow-fleshed freestone at its peak in August, along with plump, vine-ripened tomatoes of various persuasions, perhaps ones you've grown yourself. Similarly, seek out the best extra virgin oil you can afford, as this is the kind of dish where you'll taste the difference.

august joy: heirloom tomatoes and peaches with burrata

SERVES 4 TO 6

1½ pounds assorted heirloom tomatoes

3 ripe peaches, pitted and sliced into wedges

8 ounces burrata cheese (about 1 ball), at room temperature

Handful opal basil leaves or piccolo verde fino basil

Leaves from 2 sprigs tarragon

2 teaspoons champagne vinegar or white balsamic vinegar

3 to 4 tablespoons extra virgin olive oil

Sea salt and freshly ground black pepper

Slice the tomatoes according to size and shape and arrange on a platter or in a shallow bowl with the sliced peaches. Tear the burrata into chunks, and scatter over the top along with any escaped cream, the basil, and most of the tarragon leaves. Whisk together the vinegar and olive oil. Add the remaining couple tarragon leaves, gently bruised to release their oils, and let marinate for a few minutes. Add a pinch of salt to the vinaigrette and drizzle over the salad. Sprinkle with more salt and freshly ground black pepper, to taste.

The nectar explodes in your mouth
and the fragrance enchants your nose,
a natural perfume that can never be captured.

–David Mas Masumoto on the Sun Crest peach, from *Epitaph for a Peach*

rustic fruit galette

This handsome, rustic, free-form pie with a sweet cornmeal-rich dough is my favorite fallback dessert, something even the French make at home. It is really no fuss at all, and the results are delicious and beautiful. Simply layer a dough round with a bit of preserves or toasted chopped nuts to seal the crust, arrange fruit on top, and sprinkle with sugar to taste. Then fold in the edges and bake. Part of the galette's charm is that it doesn't have to be perfect. Below are two of my favorite variations; use the filling measurements as a guide, not a rule. You can also make 5 or 6 individual galettes or hand pies, baking them for 12 to 15 minutes, until golden.

SERVES 8 TO 10

½ recipe Sable Dough (page 122),
  using ½ cup cornmeal in place of
  ½ cup of the flour (in full recipe),
  at room temperature

Roll the dough out to roughly a 12-inch circle; transfer to a paper-lined sheet tray. Preheat the oven to 375°F.

Peach and Blueberry with Vanilla Bean

Slice about 3 large, firm but ripe peaches into wedges and toss in a bowl with a large handful of fresh blueberries. Scrape in the seeds from 1 vanilla bean, along with a squeeze of lemon juice, and toss to coat well. Pile the fruit onto the center of the pastry dough, leaving about 2 inches free all the way around. Sprinkle with ¼ to ⅓ cup turbinado sugar, more if you like it sweeter. Gently fold the edges in over the fruit, patching any holes by pinching those parts of the dough together. Dot the fruit with 2 teaspoons softened butter. Sprinkle a little more sugar on the edge of the crust. Bake until the crust is golden and the fruit is tender and bubbling in the center, about 45 minutes. Brush a tablespoon of warm apricot jam, thinned with a little water or brandy, over the top of the fruit after removing the galette from the oven. Cool slightly before serving.

Apricot or Prune with Amaretto

Quarter a dozen or so apricots or prunes (like Damson plums or French prunes) and toss in a bowl with a jigger of amaretto liqueur and ¼ cup turbinado sugar. Macerate for at least 20 minutes. If using apricots, spread a thin layer of Blenheim Apricot Preserves (page 108) onto the center of the dough, leaving about 2 inches free all the way around. Pile the fruit on top, scraping in the juices. Gently fold the edges in over the fruit, patching any holes by pinching those parts of the dough together. Dot the fruit with 2 teaspoons softened butter and sprinkle a small handful of sliced almonds over the top. Sprinkle a little more sugar on the edge of the crust. Bake until the crust is golden and the fruit is tender and bubbling in the center, 30 to 40 minutes. This tart tends to juice up more than others; spoon any leaking juices back over the fruit as it cooks. If desired, brush the fruit with more amaretto after removing from the oven. Cool slightly before serving.

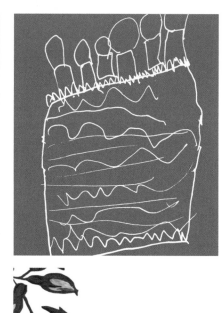

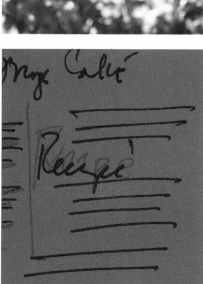

I can't say enough about this spiced chutney, which is so intoxicatingly fragrant when bubbling away. Especially since I was not terribly partial to chutney in the first place—that is, until I made my own, on a whim, for my birthday and served it with sheep's milk cheese and salumi under the shade of a California oak tree. Everyone went crazy for it; perhaps it was the mood or even the place that afternoon. Even so, I've made it several times since, with slight variations (it's quite forgiving) and loved it more each time.

Stir some through a pot of saffron-scented rice flecked with bits of roasted chicken, cilantro leaves, and toasted pine nuts or almonds for a delicious meal on the fly. It also goes well with grilled chicken and lamb kabobs. Best after it ages for a week or longer.

MAKES 1 LARGE JAR

1 pound apricots, preferably Blenheim, pitted and diced

12 sun-dried golden apricots, thinly sliced

1 mango, peeled, pitted, and diced

1 onion, chopped

2 large whole cloves garlic, finely chopped

1 red chile pepper, finely chopped, or 1 dried chile, torn (remove the seeds on either for less heat)

Grated zest of 1 lime

2-inch piece fresh ginger, finely grated

½ cinnamon stick

½ teaspoon coriander seed, cracked

½ teaspoon mustard seed

2 whole cloves, or pinch dried cloves

Few grinds freshly ground black pepper

¾ cup turbinado sugar

½ cup champagne vinegar

Combine all the ingredients in a heavy-bottomed pot and bring to a boil. Decrease the heat to low and simmer, partially covered and occasionally stirring, for 45 to 60 minutes, until the flavors meld. Most of the liquid should have evaporated. If not, cook uncovered for 5 minutes towards the end, stirring frequently so that it doesn't burn. Let sit overnight as is.

Make any desired adjustments to the spiciness the following day. Reheat, cooking a little longer for more depth of flavor as you like it. Pot into a sterilized quart-size jar. Keep on the counter for a week so the flavors develop, and then refrigerate for longer storage. It should keep for several months. Serve at room temperature along with select meats and cheese as part of a ploughman's lunch (page 67) or a late summer supper out in the orchard.

Blenheim apricots bathed in a Moscato wine syrup pair beautifully with orange-saffron panna cotta (Italian for "cooked cream"). Even better when served with Orange Pistachio Sables (page 11). The recipe for apricots makes more than you will need here, but they can sit for months in the refrigerator and only get better with age. The panna cotta needs about 3 hours to set–it should be silky smooth and near trembling on the plate to serve, hence the scant amount of gelatin. You can substitute whole milk or crème fraîche for the buttermilk, if preferred.

buttermilk panna cotta with moscato apricots

SERVES 4 TO 6,
DEPENDING ON SIZE OF MOLDS

Apricots in Syrup
2 pounds apricots, halved (4 pits reserved)

1 cup Moscato wine

1 cup water

Scant 1 cup sugar

2 tablespoons orange flower honey or other light honey

4 cardamom pods, cracked

1 vanilla bean, split

2 (1-inch) strips lemon peel

Panna Cotta
1 2/3 cups heavy cream

1/4 cup vanilla sugar

1 (1/2-inch) strip orange peel

Pinch saffron, crumbled

Dash salt

1 1/3 cups buttermilk

Scant 1 1/2 teaspoons granulated gelatin

2 tablespoons orange flower honey

2 teaspoons orange flower water

Handful pistachios or almonds, lightly toasted and chopped, for garnish

To prepare the apricots, crack open the pits, using a hammer or back of a heavy frying pan to get at the kernels. Soak the kernels in water for 15 minutes. In a saucepot, bring the wine, water, sugar, honey, and cardamom to a boil. Scrape in the vanilla seeds, and drop in the pod and the kernels. Simmer over low heat for 10 minutes. Add the apricots and poach for 2 minutes, until they just begin to soften.

Transfer the apricots with a slotted spoon to a glass bowl. Bring the wine syrup back to a boil and simmer rapidly until thick and syrupy, about 15 minutes more. Pour the hot syrup and spices over the apricots. Chill thoroughly before serving.

To make the panna cotta, heat the cream, sugar, orange peel, saffron, and salt in a small saucepan to just under a boil. Remove from the heat, cover, and steep for 30 minutes.

Place the cold buttermilk in a bowl and sprinkle with the gelatin, swirling a few times until dissolved. Rewarm the custard and stir in the buttermilk mixture and the honey. Bring to a boil and cook for 2 minutes, until it begins to thicken. Strain the custard into a bowl set over ice. Whisk a few times, until cool. Stir in the orange flower water.

Transfer the custard to a measuring cup and divide evenly among 4 to 6 molds– teacups work well–or other shallow ramekins. Cover with plastic wrap and chill until set.

To unmold, wrap a warm towel around the bottom of each cup or ramekin for 30 seconds or so, then slide the tip of a thin knife around the edges of the custard to loosen from inside the bowl. Turn over onto chilled plates.

Spoon 2 to 3 poached apricot halves around the custards, drizzling each with some syrup. Dust a bit of chopped pistachio over the top of each.

fruit sauces

A fresh fruit sauce–a few squirts of a lavish, raspberry-red currant sauce or perhaps a touch of apricot sauce–accompanying a slice of cake or drizzled over ice cream can elevate just about any dessert, and is quick and easy to make as well.

A basic no-cook method is to puree fresh fruit in a blender, adding just enough water (about 2 table-spoons per cup of fruit is a good place to start) to blend without overly thinning. (One cup of fruit will yield about ½ cup puree.) Push the puree through a fine sieve to remove any seeds and skin. Then lightly sweeten with sifted confectioners' sugar to taste, and add a squeeze of lemon juice for balance.

For a cooked berry sauce, like the blueberry sauce page 9, yielding about 1 cup, simmer 1 cup lightly crushed fruit with about ½ cup of water until soft. Then push through a fine sieve to remove any seeds. Return the sauce to medium heat, whisk in a few tablespoons of granulated sugar, and simmer until it is slightly syrupy. Stir in lemon juice or other flavorings to taste, along with ½ cup more whole or sliced berries (optional). Cook 1 minute more. To keep a cooked fruit sauce bright and reminiscent of the fruit it is, don't overcook it, and use little sweetener.

Kiwis are the one fruit I don't put in a blender, but rather puree in a food processor to avoid mashing the seeds, which can blacken the sauce. Push the puree through a sieve to remove all seeds, or simply use as is. Sweeten with sifted confectioners' sugar.

To make a smooth passion fruit sauce, scoop out the pulp and press through a sieve, pushing on the seeds to extract as much juice and flavor as possible. Warm over low heat with a little sugar or honey and the seeds of a fresh vanilla bean. It's divine over vanilla ice cream.

A breezy, refreshing dessert combining summer peaches with late-season Kadota figs, treasured for their honey-like taste. Use any flavorful peach with robust flavor, like Sun Crest, and marinate for at least 2 hours or up to overnight before serving with a floating cloud of lightly sweetened cream or Crème Fraîche Ice Cream (page 150). This is also a fine way to prepare mango slices, dressed up with fresh passion fruit and raspberries.

honey-lime peaches with crème fraîche clouds

SERVES 4 TO 6

Combine the honey, orange zest, lime zest, lime juice, cinnamon stick, and 2 tablespoons water in a medium saucepot; bring to a boil and simmer until syrupy, about 5 minutes. Let cool. Strain over the sliced peaches in a bowl. Add the vanilla bean, cover, and marinate for several hours in the refrigerator.

Just before serving, whip the cream to soft peaks, and then fold into the crème fraîche, dusting with confectioners' sugar to taste.

Arrange the marinated peach slices and figs in shallow bowls and add enough syrup to barely cover. Top each serving with a cloud of whipped crème fraîche. Garnish with more lime zest or mint leaves.

⅔ cup light-colored honey, like orange blossom honey from California

Grated zest of 1 orange

Grated zest of 1 lime

½ cup fresh lime juice

1 cinnamon stick

3 peaches, peeled, pitted, and sliced (see page 102)

1 vanilla bean, split lengthwise

½ cup heavy cream

½ cup crème fraîche

Confectioners' sugar, for dusting

About 6 Kadota or other green figs, quartered

Additional lime zest, or slivered mint leaves, for garnish

Native to China, the peach is symbolic of long life in Chinese culture and seen as the fruit of happiness and riches in Korea. In Vietnam, peach blossoms symbolize the start of spring. Its botanical name (persica) actually derives from an early belief that the fruit came from Persia, where it has flourished since ancient times.

plum gorgeous almond tart

Sweet juicy plums encased in a buttery almond cream are simply too perfect to ignore, fabulously rich without being cloying and gorgeous to look at. I've used firm but ripe plums with rosy centers here for visual effect, although any plum variety will do. In the fall, substitute the plums with sliced vanilla-poached pears or figs, brushing the fruit with a little of the poaching syrup as the tart comes out of the oven. The dough is enough for two tarts; freeze half for another use, like for my Rustic Fruit Galette (page 112).

MAKES ONE 9- OR 10-INCH TART

Sable Dough
3 cups flour

⅓ cup sugar

1 cup (2 sticks) butter, slightly softened

1 egg yolk

3 to 6 tablespoons heavy cream or cold water

Filling
1 cup whole almonds, blanched

¾ cup plus 2 tablespoons sugar

¾ cup (1½ sticks) butter, cut into 12 pieces and slightly softened

4 eggs

¼ cup flour

1 tablespoon brandy or orange liqueur, plus more for brushing

¼ to ⅓ cup plum or raspberry jam

About 8 firm but ripe plums, halved and pitted

To make the dough, combine the flour, sugar, and butter in the bowl of a food processor; pulse until the butter resembles coarse crumbs. Add the yolk and process until combined. Add the cream, a little at a time, and process until the dough just comes together. Transfer to a lightly floured board and gently knead to bring it together. Divide the dough into 2 disks, wrapping both in plastic, and freeze one for another use. Chill the other disk for 30 minutes before rolling out.

Roll the dough disk into a 12-inch circle on a lightly floured board. Carefully transfer to a 9- or 10-inch tart pan with a removable bottom, pressing any remaining bits and pieces into the edge so that it is a little thicker on the sides. Don't worry if the dough breaks as you transfer it; simply press the remaining dough into the pan, and/or patch the torn areas with scraps. Prick the bottom with a fork. Freeze the shell.

Meanwhile, to make the filling, grind the almonds with the 2 tablespoons sugar in a food processor until medium fine; you still want to see and feel the texture. Beat the remaining ¾ cup sugar with the butter in a stand mixer. Beat in the eggs, one at a time, until just blended. Beat in the ground almonds, flour, and brandy. Chill the filling long enough for it to firm up just a bit, about 20 minutes.

Preheat the oven to 350°F.

Spread a thin layer of jam (a scant ¼ cup or so) on the bottom of the uncooked tart shell and spread the almond filling over the top. Gently push the plum halves, cut side up, into the filling. Brush the plums with a little brandy. Bake for 50 to 60 minutes, until the filling is golden brown and set in the middle. Cool on a rack before carefully removing the tart from the pan. Warm any remaining jam with a little water to make a thin glaze and brush over the tart before serving.

NOTE: You can also make this tart with blackberries, scattering a few into the batter before it cooks, then topping the baked tart with fresh berries to serve.

Do not let the peasant know how good cheese is with pears.

—Italian proverb

4
beauty
& windfall

Fruits of Love and Longing

fall fruits

Like a 16th-century Caravaggio painting, late summer and early fall bring together a still life of gorgeous fruits in earthy colors and voluptuous shapes: fleshy melons and inviting figs; apples, pears, and quince—the fruits of love and longing—with flecks of gold and green; deep orange persimmons; leathery-skinned ruby pomegranates; and a plethora of plump grapes in a variety of colors clustered at the stem. There is hardly a moment to catch one's breath amidst a sudden windfall of orchard fruits. The autumn harvest seems to be my un-doing, when nature makes its last harried push and we rush to plunder the vines. When the mountains turn flaxen and the days begin to shorten is when I long for home again, to walk the dusty roads and sip scarlet wine overlooking the sea. I remember making slow-cooked apple butter using the burnished beauties from Kate's tree, gathering storied quince from the neighbor's and bathing them in wine and sugar, until they turned a pinkish hue and permeat-ed the house with their musky scent. Filling the bowl at my table with splitting pomegranate, I recall the ancient story of Persephone in the underworld, of a woman's longing and anticipa-tion of spring. The jewel-like seeds are just the things for brightening a salad, scattering over a dessert, or drowning in a glass of blush juice with a spoonful of sugar. Shapely pears offer up their own symbols—of luxurious pleasure most of all—each with a unique flavor and profile.

I love the full-figured buttery Comice pears for making a marmalade-like butter (see page 148). The harder, earthier Boscs are ideal for roasting with sherry or nibbling with a bit of salty sheep's milk cheese. Choose smaller, sweet Seckel pears for poaching whole in wine, a lovely sight indeed. We take apples for granted most of the year, but it's now when they are at their best and more true to their heritage. Look for firm, unwaxed apples—local heirlooms from nearby are always a good bet—with gorgeous striping and mixed shades of green, yellow, and red for a variety of uses: tarts, ices, puddings, and pies.

September in California is typically bursting at the seams with sweet melons, late-season figs, and an array of herbs, vine tomatoes, and wild greens. What better than to combine them in a gorgeous composed salad? Oloroso sherry is the surprise ingredient in the dressing, enhancing the finished dish. In a pinch, use fine-quality sherry wine vinegar instead—though a little less of it—and a pinch of sugar.

september salad

SERVES 4 TO 6
AS A STARTER COURSE

1 ripe heirloom melon

About ⅓ pound thinly sliced prosciutto

8 to 12 ripe figs (about 1 basket), halved

Handful of wild or young arugula leaves

Opal basil leaves

Spearmint leaves

Handful of almonds, lightly toasted and sliced

½ cup vine-ripened cherry tomatoes

About ¼ cup oloroso sherry

Extra virgin olive oil

Coarse sea salt and freshly ground black pepper

Peel, seed, and thinly slice the melon (use only half if it is substantial), then arrange the slices on a large platter. Drape the prosciutto over the top and scatter with the figs, arugula, and a few leaves each of basil and spearmint, torn or slivered if they are large. Sprinkle with the almonds and a few tomatoes. Warm the sherry in a small pan over low heat for just a minute. Transfer to a small bowl, and then swirl in olive oil to taste. Drizzle over the salad. Season with sea salt and freshly ground black pepper.

A comforting grilled ham and cheese sandwich turns divine with a figgy relish and other quality ingredients. You can interpret this sandwich any way you like, but I am fond of it with thin slices of prosciutto and buttery Toma cheese, a semi-hard cow's milk cheese from the Aosta region of Italy. Sprinkle with a dusting of Parmesan just before serving. The relish can be made ahead and kept in the refrigerator, and makes more than you will need. Reserve any extra to enjoy with cheese and wine in the afternoon. It will keep for several months in the refrigerator.

fig relish and ham sandwiches (panini)

MAKES 2 SANDWICHES, SERVING 2 TO 4

2 artisanal rolls, or 4 slices ciabatta bread

Sweet butter

Toma cheese, sliced or grated

Several thin slices prosciutto

Basil leaves

Arugula

Fig Relish (recipe follows)

Olive oil or butter

Grated Parmesan cheese, for garnish

Slice the rolls lengthwise and spread a little sweet butter on the bottom halves. Layer each with some cheese, a few slices of prosciutto, and a couple basil leaves along with a tussle of arugula. Spread a generous amount of fig relish on the top half of each roll, then place on top of the layered half. Gently press down to adhere.

Heat a cast-iron pan over medium-low heat and lightly brush with olive oil or a little butter. Add one or two sandwiches at a time and cook until lightly browned on one side. Brush the tops with a little more oil and turn over. Place a pot lid or heavy plate on top and gently press down as they cook. Cook until the cheese is melted and the roll is nicely browned and crusty. To serve, slice each sandwich in half on the diagonal and dust with a small amount of Parmesan cheese.

fig relish

MAKES ABOUT 1 CUP

1 basket Kadota or Mission figs (about ½ pound), stemmed and peeled

½ cup sugar

½ cup apple cider vinegar or champagne vinegar

1 teaspoon mustard seed

Pinch salt

About 1 teaspoon dry mustard (optional)

Coarsely chop the figs and place in a small pot with the sugar, vinegar, mustard seed, salt, and ¼ cup water. Bring to a boil over medium heat and simmer, stirring on occasion, for 20 minutes, until it resembles a loose jam. Stir in the dry mustard to taste, if using. Transfer to a glass bowl or jar. Refrigerate once cool.

honey-baked figs with lavender and wine

love this dish: It exudes everything this book is about, the pleasures and beauty of ripe fruit simply prepared. Baking figs brings out their natural, honey sweetness, and the wine creates a lovely drizzling sauce that adds to the allure. Look for firm but ripe figs that ooze lusciousness, and use a medium-dry white or red wine to complement. Later in the season, I might make this with Marsala or Port, but too much of either can mask the flavors of the figs themselves, as both are quite sweet and rich. Serve these figs as dessert with a little crème fraîche (or ice cream) or as is to accompany a cheese course. A soft, unctuous goat cheese or fresh ricotta would be divine. Drizzle the cheese and the figs with some of the juices when serving.

SERVES 4

6 or so fresh figs

Sea salt

2 teaspoons butter

About 2 tablespoons orange blossom honey, or something more robust depending on the occasion

Generous ½ glass wine

Pinch dried lavender flowers

Preheat the oven to 375°F.

Halve the figs and scatter in a baking dish. Sprinkle with a little sea salt and dot with the butter. Gently warm the honey and drizzle over the figs, then pour the wine over all. Sprinkle with lavender flowers to taste. Roast the figs until they look and feel fairly soft and the juices begin to leak, 12 to 15 minutes. Serve warm or at room temperature.

pear and butternut squash soup

At the first sign of a rain or a blustery wind in the heart of fall, nothing says home like a warming squash soup. Pears (or apples) add a natural sweetness to the soup and contribute to its velvety smooth texture once incorporated. Garnish with toasted rounds of bread smeared with a little blue cheese for a fancier affair, or simply with lightly whisked cream or a dollop of plain yogurt.

SERVES 4 TO 6

1 medium butternut or kabocha squash, halved and seeded

1 tablespoon olive oil or butter

1 yellow onion, chopped

1 carrot, peeled and chopped

1 clove garlic, finely chopped

1 to 2 teaspoons curry powder

About a 1-inch piece fresh ginger, peeled and finely grated

2 Bosc pears, peeled, cored, and chopped

4 cups good-quality chicken stock or water, plus more to thin

Salt and freshly ground black pepper

Preheat the oven to 400°F.

Cut the squash into large chunks and arrange in a casserole dish or deep baking pan, cut sides down. Add about ¼ cup water, enough to wet the bottom of the pan. Cover tightly with foil and roast for 45 minutes to 1 hour, until the flesh is soft.

Heat the oil in a heavy pot over medium heat. Add the onion, carrot, and garlic and cook until lightly browned, about 5 minutes. Stir in the curry powder and fresh ginger. Add the squash, pears, chicken stock, and a pinch of salt. Cook until the carrots and pears are soft and the flavors have fully melded, 20 to 25 minutes. Cool slightly, then puree in a blender, or use an immersion mixer, blending right in the pot (off the heat). Reheat the soup and season with salt and pepper and a pinch more curry powder, to taste. Thin as needed with more chicken stock or water to reach desired consistency.

Pears and quince are lovely when cooked in wine syrup, and it's an easy way to put them up for another use. These are good served chilled as a light dessert with custard, or later sliced and used in a cake or tart (such as my plum tart, on page 122). Quince will take more time to cook than pears and tend to turn the liquid a gorgeous, rosy hue. It's easier to peel quince after they've been cut.

wine- poached fall fruit

My basic method (for 4 to 6 pears or quince) is to combine about 1 cup each dessert wine (like vin santo) and water with ½ to ⅔ cup sugar or honey, a cinnamon stick and star anise, a few peppercorns, a bay leaf, a split vanilla bean, and a strip or two of lemon peel. (For a savory dish, perhaps use a fruity red wine and only ½ cup sugar and omit or add spices accordingly.) Bring to a simmer in a saucepot over medium-high heat and cook for about 5 minutes.

Peel, halve, and core the fruit, unless poaching whole like you might with Seckel pears. Add the fruit to the pot and press a piece of parchment on top to keep it immersed. Decrease the heat to medium and gently poach until just tender, 15 to 20 minutes for pears, depending on size and ripeness, and longer for quince. Remove from the heat and cool the fruit in the syrup. Refrigerate, spooning out the fruit as needed.

You can use this same liquid and method to poach a selection of dried fruits, such as pears, prunes, and figs, to accompany a cheese course; reduce the syrup by half for drizzling.

Aged sherry finds its match in roasted pears and voluptuous sabayon custard, while a huckleberry sauce brings it all together. This is one of those ethereal desserts, lovely in every way and quite simple to put together. Use an assortment of pears, like Bosc or Forelle (shown), for a variety of textures and tastes, and don't skimp on the quality of the sherry if you can help it.

sherry-roasted pears with huckleberry sauce and sabayon

SERVES 4 TO 6

Pears
4 to 6 pears, halved and cored
⅓ cup oloroso sherry
1 vanilla bean, split lengthwise
2 tablespoons honey
1 tablespoon butter

Sabayon
4 egg yolks
¼ cup oloroso sherry
3 tablespoons sugar
1 tablespoon honey
½ cup heavy cream, whipped

Huckleberry Sauce
4 ounces huckleberries (about 1 cup)
2 tablespoons sugar
2 tablespoons honey
1 teaspoon pure vanilla extract
1 teaspoon fresh lemon juice

Preheat the oven to 375°F.

To roast the pears, place in a baking dish, cut sides up. Pour the sherry over the top. Scrape in the vanilla seeds and drop in the pod; drizzle with the honey and dot with the butter. Roast, basting a few times with the juices, for 20 to 30 minutes, until the pears are just tender and golden. Turn them over at any point if they seem to be browning too quickly.

Meanwhile, to make the sabayon, whisk the egg yolks, sherry, sugar, and honey in a heatproof bowl over a gently simmering pot of water. Avoid curdling the eggs by continuously whisking and cooking over low heat until the custard is thick and easily coats the back of a spoon. It should be near double in volume. Place over a bowl of ice and continue to whisk until cool. Fold in the cream.

To make the huckleberry sauce, combine half of the huckleberries with ¼ cup water, the sugar, honey, vanilla extract, and lemon juice in a small saucepot over medium heat. Bring to a simmer and cook for about 5 minutes, until slightly thickened. Press through a sieve, pushing on the berries to extract as much juice as possible. Return to low heat. Stir in the remaining berries and cook for 2 minutes. Cool to room temperature.

Arrange the pears in a serving bowl and spoon any juices over the top. Drizzle the pears with the berry sauce and dollop with sabayon.

By late autumn, ripples of fog move in and out across the tawny, sun-scorched hills, leaves fall away, and we're given crisp airy evenings after lengthy days of sunshine and collecting fruit. Even then, the kids push to be outside every chance they get, to splash through the first mud puddles and challenge the wind as they trudge up the hills to a neighbor's, cold dewy fog kissing their cheeks a rosy hue. In the mountains, you can almost taste the brisk air, feel it through your body as Indian summer turns its delirious head, hastening autumn and calling for winter to bring on the rain. So we soldier on, taking leisurely walks below moody skies, gathering leaves, twigs, and stones, foraging for fruit: the last of the purple plums to a new crop of figs at the top of the hill; tart-sweet pink apples no bigger than a child's fist and Seckel pears from the orchard at Molera; heart-shaped persimmons and ruby pomegranates arouse a splash of brilliant orange and deep crimson for the table; golden quince perfume the house with their intoxicating scent, breathing sweet life into my hours of questioning, each moment of longing.

pouissons with honey, wine, and quince

*P*ouissons *(small chickens) bathed in honey, wine, and brandy with aromatic quince and herbs may seem decadent and fairytale-like, but they are not as boozy and over the top as the ingredients might suggest. And besides, they are incredibly delicious. Dress up or down, no matter, but be sure to baste the birds as they cook with some of the quince poaching liquid to achieve a lacquered skin and help bring the flavors together.*

SERVES 2 TO 4

2 *pouissons* (about 1 pound each)

Coarse sea salt

½ cup honey

Pinch saffron

4 rosemary sprigs

1 lemon

2 quince, peeled, cored, and sliced into thick wedges

About 2 tablespoons orange flower water

2 cloves garlic

2 to 3 tablespoons butter

1 cup dry white wine

¼ cup brandy

Rinse the *pouissons* inside and out and pat dry. Rub the skin with a generous amount of sea salt, loosely cover with plastic wrap, and leave at room temperature for about an hour before cooking.

Meanwhile, poach the quince. In a saucepan, bring 2 cups water (or half water and wine), the honey, saffron, 1 sprig of rosemary, and the juice of the lemon plus a strip of peel to a simmer over medium-high heat. Add the quince (and a few skins—they give it a rosy hue). Decrease the heat to medium and gently poach until the quince are just tender, about 25 minutes. Remove from the heat; stir in orange flower water to taste.

Preheat the oven to 400°F.

Tuck a garlic clove into the cavity of each bird, along with a pinch of salt and a rosemary sprig. Rub the butter into the skin of each bird. Place breast side up in a baking dish and sprinkle with coarsely chopped rosemary leaves. Pour the wine and brandy over the top, along with a few spoonfuls of the quince poaching liquid.

Place the pan on the top rack of the oven and roast the *pouissons* for 15 minutes. Turn the birds over and roast for 15 minutes more, all the while basting with the juices. Turn the *pouissons* back over (breast up). Add the poached quince slices to the pan. Baste again with both the juices and the poaching liquid. Continue cooking and basting until the chicken is golden and the thigh juices run clear when pricked with a fork, about 30 minutes more.

Transfer the *pouissons* to a serving platter and loosely cover. Pour some of the juices from the pan into a small saucepot and skim off the fat. Simmer rapidly until slightly syrupy. Add some of the quince poaching liquid, to taste. Serve the *pouissons* with the juices and the quince.

quince

Quince is one of those mystery fruits, ethereal and intoxicatingly fragrant when ripe, and yet inedible in its raw state and somewhat intimidating to work with. A few in a bowl at the table have the power to perfume a whole room and transcend the feeling of time and place, but few know what to do with them. I didn't the first time I came across quince. They are squash-hard with a yellow to chartreuse furry outer skin (often rubbed off when purchased at the store) and resemble an oddly shaped apple. The golden quince is thought to be the original forbidden fruit, devoured by Eve in the Garden of Eden. It turns a burnt ruby orange when cooked with sugar, and is the basis for *membrillo*, a firm marmalade popular in Spain, where it is served with sheep's milk cheese.

This Spanish preserve combines quince with rose geranium leaf. Both share a similar scent—a little tropical, pineapple, and rose all in one. My recipe manages to forgo the days-long outdoor sunning of the traditional membrillo recipe. Some recipes recommend cooking the thickened paste in a low-temperature oven for several hours to achieve a solid paste, but if you cook it on the stove long enough, it does fine to set up on its own over several days at room temperature. Use equal amounts of sugar and quince pulp for either method below.

quince
with rose
geranium

MAKES ABOUT 4 CUPS

5 or 6 quince
Sugar
Lemon juice
Rose geranium leaves
Rose water (optional)

Peel the quince and halve and core the fruit, reserving about half of the peel and all the seeds. Wrap the peel and the seeds in a piece of cheesecloth and tie securely at the top. Cut the quince into small chunks and place in a heavy pot along with the cheesecloth bundle. Add 4 to 6 cups water, just enough to cover. Place a round of parchment on the quince to help keep the fruit moist and partially submerged as it cooks. Cook the quince over medium-low heat until very soft, about an hour or often longer, adding more liquid as needed to prevent scorching.

To make a firm *membrillo* paste, drain off any liquid that remains (or reserve to make a jelly or syrup; simply cook the liquid with an equal amount of sugar). Discard the skins and seeds. Mash the fruit and push through a sieve, or puree it. Measure the pulp and return to the pot. For every 1 cup of pulp, add 1 cup of sugar, the juice of ½ lemon, and 1 geranium leaf.

Cook the quince and sugar over low heat, stirring fairly frequently, until it turns a deep, ruby orange—the color change is quite noticeable the longer it cooks—and seems fairly firm, about an hour or longer. Watch it closely so that it doesn't scorch. Remove the geranium leaf and stir in a couple drops of rose water, if you like, to taste. Pour the paste into a lightly oiled mold or small loaf pan. Cover with parchment and leave at room temperature for a few days, until fully set. Unmold and wrap in plastic. Store in the refrigerator or in a cool area of the cupboard.

To make a loose marmalade, don't drain the quince after cooking, but mash or puree the fruit with the water. Proceed to measure and add the sugar and other ingredients, as above. Then cook over low heat, stirring on occasion, until it turns a deep rosy pink, about 30 minutes. For a dense marmalade, as shown in the picture—though not quite a paste—continue cooking another 15 minutes or so. I like to cook it a fairly long time to achieve depth of flavor and a firm but still spreadable texture. You will note a change in the color, from pink to ruby as it caramelizes. Pour the cooked quince into sterilized jars, cover with lids, and turn over to set. Serve with aged sheep's milk cheese.

For me, the scent of quince takes me back to living at Henry Miller's house on Partington Ridge where I first discovered the fruit and what to do with it. I made my first batch of membrillo on a tiny gas stove in a painterly kitchen with sunny yellow walls, following a traditional recipe from a friend's mother in Portugal.

slow cooked apple butter

I made my best apple butter yet–60 jars plus–using a windfall of striped heirloom apples I picked from Pisoni Vineyards ranch. It's hard to go wrong when you have fruit with such measurable provenance, but it also helps to cook the fruit long and slow and put a little love into the process. Some people swear by their slow cooker or even the oven method, but cooking on the stove in small batches with a patient and caring hand works for me. Consider letting the apple butter rest overnight, then bringing back to a simmer the next day before potting for greater depth of flavor. Smear the butter on toast, serve with ham, or use as the base for a classic French Apple Tart (page 151). Try this same method for making pear marmalade butter, accenting with vanilla bean or candied ginger and cooking for less time.

MAKES ABOUT FOUR ½-PINT JARS

3 pounds heirloom apples, peeled, cored, and cut into chunks

1¼ cups apple cider

1 cinnamon stick

2 (½-inch) strips lemon peel, plus the juice of 1 lemon

2½ to 3 cups sugar (or use a little honey in the mix)

Pinch fresh ground nutmeg

Pinch ground cinnamon

Place the apples in a large, heavy-bottomed pot with the apple cider, cinnamon stick, and lemon peel. Cook over medium heat, occasionally stirring, until the apples are soft and pulpy and most of the liquid has evaporated, about 45 minutes. If the cider evaporates before the apples are cooked through, add a little water.

Push the apples through a sieve or food mill for a smooth butter, or simply mash with the back of a wooden spoon for a chunkier texture. Discard the lemon peel and cinnamon stick. Return the pulp to the same pot. Add the lemon juice, sugar (more or less depending on the tartness of the apples), and ground spices and slowly bring to a simmer until the sugar is dissolved.

Cook over medium heat for about 15 minutes, stirring constantly. Take care to use a long wooden spoon and perhaps wear gloves, as any splatters do burn. Reduce the heat to low and continue cooking and stirring until the butter is thick and syrupy and a golden straw-like color, about 45 minutes. If you like it more caramelized, as I do, continue cooking for another 15 minutes or so. Watch it closely at this point, as the bottom of the pot can easily scorch and ruin your hard work. If this does happen, turn off the heat immediately and quickly pour the butter into a new pot, leaving the scorched areas in the former pot. Ladle the apple butter into hot, sterilized jars, cover with lids, turn over, and let stand overnight.

cider-braised heirloom apples with crème fraîche ice cream

This is a comforting and homey dessert that takes baked apples to new heights. Choose a smaller, crisp, red-tinged heirloom baking apple, like Gravenstein, for the best results and visual appeal. Serve warm with crème fraîche ice cream or simply with the braising juices, simmered with a little heavy cream to make a caramel. Sprinkle with toasted, sweetened bread crumbs, like a "Betty" topping, or walnuts, for a festive finish.

SERVES 4 TO 6

½ cup apple cider

2 tablespoons brown sugar

2 tablespoons honey

1½ tablespoons butter

1 tablespoon apple cider vinegar

½ cinnamon stick

2 juniper berries

4 heirloom apples, halved and cored, skin and stem left on

Crème Fraîche Ice Cream

2 cups half-and-half

½ cup sugar

1 tablespoon honey

1 vanilla bean, split lengthwise

5 egg yolks, lightly beaten

1 cup crème fraîche

Preheat the oven to 375°F.

Bring the apple cider, sugar, honey, butter, vinegar, cinnamon, and juniper to a simmer in a small saucepot over medium heat. Cook until reduced by nearly half.

Place the apples cut side down in a small baking dish. Pour the cider syrup over the apples. Braise in the oven, uncovered and occasionally basting with syrup, for 20 to 30 minutes, until the apples are just tender. Turn the apples over and cook for 5 minutes longer to brown. Transfer the apples to a serving dish. Pour the juices back into the saucepot and reduce over medium-high heat until thick and syrupy. Pour over the apples and serve with the ice cream.

For the ice cream, combine the half-and-half, sugar, honey, and vanilla pod and seeds in a saucepot over medium heat. Bring to just under a boil, stirring to dissolve the sugar, then remove from the heat. Cover and steep for 20 minutes.

Remove the vanilla pod and return the pot to medium-low heat. Place the beaten yolks in a medium bowl and temper them by stirring in one-third of the hot cream mixture, then pouring the mixture back into the pot. Cook, stirring, until the mixture coats the back of a spoon, about 5 minutes. Pour into a bowl set over ice and stir in the crème fraîche. Chill thoroughly.

Churn in an ice cream maker, then harden in the freezer before serving.

There is nothing in the world more peaceful than apple-leaves with an early moon.

–Alice Meynell

french apple tart

A country-style apple tart consisting solely of sliced apples and sugar in a rich pastry is one of my favorite desserts, a classic from the French home kitchen. A thin layer of cooked apples (or apple butter) or quince spread beneath the apples offers a nice change of landscape. But the "simpler the better" says my French stepmother, remarking on the classic tart from her childhood, and I tend to agree. The whole point is to not have to fuss over it much. I make a pâte brisée–short crust dough–by hand using an old-fashioned pastry cutter, but you are welcome to use a food processor–just don't overwork it.

MAKES ONE 8- OR 9-INCH TART

Short Crust Dough
1 cup flour

2 teaspoons sugar

Pinch salt

½ cup (1 stick) cold butter, cut into small pieces

2 to 3 tablespoons ice water

Filling
About ⅓ cup sugar

4 to 5 cooking apples (like Golden Delicious), peeled, cored, and thinly sliced

1 tablespoon butter

Apricot jam or jelly, for glazing

Crème fraîche, for serving

To make the dough, combine the flour, sugar, and salt in a mixing bowl. Cut in the butter using a pastry cutter or fork until the mixture resembles coarse meal. Stir in just enough ice water to begin to bring the dough together. Turn out onto a lightly floured board and gently gather into a ball. Flatten into a disk. Wrap in plastic and refrigerate for 30 minutes to relax the dough.

Roll the dough out to a 10- to 11-inch round. Fit the round in an 8- or 9-inch ring mold set on a baking sheet lined with parchment paper, or in a tart pan with a removable bottom. Fold excess dough in on itself to form a thicker edge, pressing flat to the top as you go. Prick the bottom of the tart shell all over. Chill for another 20 minutes or so.

Preheat the oven to 350°F.

To fill the tart shell, sprinkle a little sugar on the bottom. Arrange the apples in the shell, slightly fanning out in concentric circles so that they overlap. Sprinkle with more sugar and continue to layer with apples until they fill the shell. Sprinkle with a final amount of sugar and dot with the butter.

Bake the tart until the apples are tender and the crust is golden, about 45 minutes. Warm a small amount of apricot jam, thinning with a little water or brandy to make a glaze. Generously brush the apples with the glaze as the tart comes out the oven. Serve warm or at room temperature with a dollop of crème fraîche.

Bright and mildly acidic pomegranate marries beautifully with rich meats. It is often paired with lamb in the Middle East, where both the fruit and pomegranate molasses (a syrup made by cooking down the seeds and juice) are popular in cooked dishes. Inspired by that part of the world, I've combined them with lavender flowers in a marinade for lamb chops. The fusion of flavors is a little eccentric for the uninitiated palate and may take you by surprise, so give it a moment to linger on the tongue. Serve the chops with a few leaves of arugula and couscous or other grain to round out the meal. You will want 2 or 3 chops per person, depending on their size. Have the butcher split and "French" a lamb rack for you, or chose loin chops. The marinade would also be lovely rubbed into a leg of lamb, then slow roasted in the oven or on a spit.

grilled lamb chops with pomegranate

SERVES 2 TO 4

Loin or rib chops, enough to serve

Salt and freshly ground black pepper

3 tablespoons olive oil

2 tablespoons fresh lemon juice, plus more as needed

1 tablespoon pomegranate molasses

1 small shallot, finely chopped

1 clove garlic, minced

2 teaspoons chopped fresh rosemary

1 teaspoon dried lavender flowers

Seeds from 1 small pomegranate

Handful arugula leaves

Trim any excess fat or gristle from the chops. Season with salt and pepper. Place in a shallow glass baking dish.

Whisk the olive oil, lemon juice, pomegranate molasses, shallot, garlic, rosemary, lavender, pinch of salt, and pepper to taste in a small bowl. Pour about half of the marinade over the chops. Loosely cover and set aside for an hour, turning to coat both sides once or twice during that time. Add half the pomegranate seeds to the remaining marinade, adding in a little more lemon juice to make it more like vinaigrette. Set aside.

Heat a stovetop grill pan or cast-iron skillet to medium-high. Add the chops and cook to desired doneness, 3 to 4 minutes per side for medium-rare. Arrange on plates with a few leaves of arugula tucked underneath. Drizzle with the reserved marinade and scatter the remaining pomegranate seeds over the tops.

fall salad with smoked trout, apples, and pomegranate

Earthy, golden beets and crisp-tart apples are a classic combination turned stellar when tangled with gorgeous fall greens, flecks of salty trout, and vibrant pomegranate seeds–a painter's salad indeed. The crème fraîche adds just the right amount of creaminess to the dressing without overdoing it. If you prefer something lighter, substitute plain yogurt for the crème fraîche, or dress the salad with a simple cider vinaigrette instead.

SERVES 4

Beets

1 bunch baby golden or Chiogga beets, trimmed and cleaned

Olive oil

Salt and freshly ground black pepper

Dressing

⅓ cup crème fraîche

1 small shallot, minced

1 tablespoon finely chopped parsley

1 tablespoon finely chopped dill

1 to 2 tablespoons fresh lemon juice

1 tablespoon extra virgin olive oil

Freshly ground white pepper

Salad

2 to 3 heads gem lettuce, rinsed

1 head Treviso or other radicchio

2 small crisp heirloom apples, cored and thinly sliced

About ½ pound smoked trout, flaked

Seeds from ½ pomegranate

⅓ cup walnuts, lightly toasted and coarsely chopped

To roast the beets, preheat the oven to 400°F. Place the beets in a small baking dish, add a splash of water, and drizzle lightly with olive oil. Cover with aluminum foil and roast for about 30 minutes, until just tender. Rub the skins off while still warm. Halve or quarter the beets, depending on the size, and then toss with a little more olive oil to coat. Lightly season with salt and pepper. Set aside.

To make the dressing, combine the crème fraîche, shallot, parsley, and dill in a small bowl. Whisk in the lemon juice and olive oil. Season with salt and white pepper to taste.

Separate the leaves of the lettuce and radicchio. Tear any of the larger radicchio leaves into smaller pieces. Pile both greens into a large bowl. Add the apples, beets, and trout and gently toss with dressing to taste. Arrange the salad on plates. Scatter with the pomegranate seeds and toasted walnuts.

Pale pink apples and fleshy persimmons appear next to the pomegranate tree, beauty of home and orchard revealing itself.

This French-style open-face sandwich is right up my alley and not so unlike what I fix for myself regularly, culling the fridge for bits of cheese, relishes, and yesterday's veggies to serve atop a slice or two of hearty toast; it gets me through the afternoon. This takes inspiration from a pan-roasted plum and chanterelle salad with bacon that I'm fond of from Danish cookbook author Trina Hahnemann. In both cases, the sweetness of the cooked fruit plays off the earthy mushrooms and salty pork—yet another sumptuous mélange to make before winter sets in.

Heat a little olive oil or butter in a small pan over medium-high heat. Add the chanterelles and garlic and sauté until the mushrooms are lightly browned and just starting to soften, about 3 minutes. Stir in the thyme and persimmon and cook and stir for 1 to 2 minutes more. Add a splash of vinegar. Give the pan a good shake to distribute the flavors and remove from the heat. Add the arugula leaves and a pinch of salt. Gently toss, using your fingers, to combine.

Meanwhile, lightly toast the bread in a toaster or the broiler. Spread each piece with some of the cheese and drape with the speck, if using. Slice the toasts in half on the diagonal and arrange on serving plates. Top each piece with an equal portion of the persimmon and mushroom mixture, allowing it to fall onto the plate, as it will anyway. Drizzle with a small amount of extra virgin olive oil, to taste, and grind a few twists of black pepper over the top.

persimmon and chanterelle tartines

SERVES 2

Olive oil or butter

⅓ pound chanterelles

1 small clove chopped garlic

Sprinkling of thyme leaves or chopped chives

1 Fuyu persimmon, peeled and sliced into thin wedges

Splash balsamic vinegar

Handful arugula leaves

Sea salt

3 slices artisanal walnut bread or other hearty country bread, lightly toasted

About ¼ cup fromage blanc or other fresh cheese like ricotta (drained of whey)

3 to 6 thin slices speck or other cured ham (optional)

Extra virgin olive oil, for drizzling

Freshly ground black pepper

Shaped more like a bar than a cookie, these have become one of those oddly comforting treats that hold a lot of dear memories. The recipe is a perennial favorite given to me by my sister Sara (one she typically throws together without measurements) for this book, and one she adapted from another family member. What I love about them—besides their chewy goodness and use of the heart-shaped persimmon at its ripest—is that they bring me back to a particular moment in time, to the innocence of childhood, and the dreams we all carried, some shared and some our very own.

sara's persimmon chocolate chip cookies

MAKES ONE 8-INCH SQUARE PAN

½ cup (1 stick) butter, at room temperature

¾ cup brown sugar

2 eggs

2 very ripe Hachiya persimmons, peeled and seeded

1 teaspoon pure vanilla extract

2 cups all-purpose flour (or use half whole-wheat flour)

1 teaspoon baking soda

½ teaspoon salt

Generous pinch ground cinnamon

Pinch nutmeg

1 cup chocolate chips

About ½ cup walnuts, coarsely chopped (optional)

Preheat the oven to 350°F. Lightly grease an 8-inch square baking pan.

Beat the butter with the sugar in a stand mixer, or by hand using a wooden spoon, until light and fluffy. Beat in the eggs. Beat in the persimmon pulp and vanilla extract. Mix the flour with the baking soda, salt, and spices. Beat into the butter mixture until just combined. Stir in the chocolate chips and walnuts, if using.

Scrape the batter into the prepared pan and bake for 20 to 25 minutes, until a toothpick inserted in the center comes out fairly clean. Cool on a rack, then cut into squares.

Pictured are Fuyu persimmons.

There was a time, for part of the year, when my sister and I lived atop the same mountain, in the same orchard, an abundance of persimmons at our reach.

tomato, grape, and ricotta flatbread

Sweet, juicy grapes meld beautifully with cherry tomatoes and fresh ricotta cheese in this rustic flatbread, my ode to California's Indian summer when both fruits are at their glorious peak. Smaller, more intensely flavored wine grapes, like Cabernet Franc (the dark purple grapes shown), are particularly sweet and intensely delicious and offer a rich study in contrasts against the medley of yellow, orange, and red tomatoes and greens. Use good-quality, stone-ground bread flour for the best results. If you have a pizza stone, by all means use it to bake this bread.

MAKES 2 OR 3 FLATBREADS

Dough
1 teaspoon active dry yeast
1 cup tepid water, plus more as needed
3 cups bread flour
1 teaspoon salt
2 tablespoons olive oil

Topping
Extra virgin olive oil
½ pound ricotta cheese (about 1 cup)
2 cups cherry tomatoes, halved
½ pound wine grapes, rinsed,
    halved, and seeded
Leaves from 2 to 3 sprigs
    rosemary, coarsely chopped
Coarse sea salt
Handful arugula,
    plus a few leaves for garnish

To make the dough, sprinkle the yeast over the water in a medium bowl and stir in 1 cup of the flour. Set aside in a warm place for 2 hours, or up to overnight. You are essentially creating a sponge or *poolish*–this slow rise ultimately results in a more complexly flavored dough.

Combine the remaining 2 cups of flour with the salt and stir into the yeast mixture, along with the olive oil, until well combined. Add up to ¼ cup more water, if needed, to achieve a dough that comes together easily. Transfer to a lightly floured board and knead for 5 minutes, until the dough feels elastic and smooth. Gather into a ball and place in a lightly oiled bowl. Cover and set aside in a warm place until doubled in size, about 1 hour.

Preheat the oven to 400°F. Line 2 or 3 baking sheets with parchment and sprinkle with cornmeal or flour.

Gently punch down the dough. Divide it into 2 or 3 balls. Take one and roll out into a loose rectangle shape about ¼ inch thick. Transfer to a prepared baking sheet. Dot the dough using your fingers, making small wells in it. Brush the surface liberally with extra virgin olive oil. Spread one-half or one-third of the ricotta on the surface and scatter with tomatoes and grapes. Sprinkle with rosemary and sea salt to taste, and a few leaves of arugula. Drizzle with a little more olive oil. Repeat with the remaining dough.

Bake until the crust is golden and the topping nicely charred, about 25 minutes. Top with more fresh arugula leaves.

Life is an orchard where the seasons stroll.

–Adonis, from "To The Poem"

postscript

I am fortunate to have been able to draw on the memory of many orchards while writing this book, in particular my friend Kate's orchard as well as the one I lived at for a summer in Bolinas, California, next door to a poet, a few years later. There we often made jam too, and pickles, and jellies, and pies. We put up fruit as it ripened and after, when it fell to the ground. We told our stories, and ate apricot jam on toast. We wrote poems; it was a beautiful thing.

As I write this, California's Indian summer has again come and gone and it is truly fall; leaves are turning auburn, and we've already had rain. The markets are laden with tawny orange persimmons, carmine pears, and crisp heirloom apples of every color. I buy the last of the plump, late-harvest figs to eat out of hand, and ponder the many tropical fruits on display. The timing is plush, ample, and full, the ripe moments before winter longing, slow growth, and retreat.

I think about what I will make in January with the few Meyer lemons that are growing on my tree, or the kumquat that I meant to plant. I recall my recent visit to Hawaii, where I once lived, the sweet, musky scent of tropical orchards, the tastes and colors of island living, and how a body shifts naturally to assimilate, to my wanting lush, spicy flavors as part of my story again.

As you leaf through *Plum Gorgeous*, I hope you will decide for yourself what recipes and tastes might reflect your own passions, your own memories and meanderings throughout the seasons of your life. There is no specific line drawn, no one moment when the seasons change, but rather a continuum, a blurring from one to the next, to muse on a sentimental passage in *Epitaph for a Peach*. It's that blur that captivates me, the nature of what's in between, the beautiful and delicious moments captured just outside the frame.

The virtue of an orchard life, as I see it after all, is the stroll, the slowing down long enough to gather fruit and put it by, to make a pear tart when you planned on making a plum one instead, or substituting persimmons for figs because one is ripe and the other is not–the unexpected is often surprising, and can be just as delicious and full. Harvesting from the orchard is as much the delight as the awakening, a reminder of life's impermanence and joy. The anticipation and wait for a particular fruit to arrive is part of the fun, part of the return to something familiar, to reflecting back on your own narrative, to being spontaneous and free.

white chocolate passion fruit truffles

White chocolate blended with heady passion fruit and pistachio is a perfect sweet ending to a meal in the orchard, and to this book, bringing so much of what I love-exotic flavors, beauty, imagination-to the table. There are several steps involved, including chilling the white chocolate filling, preferably for several hours. Use good-quality chocolate, especially for the white, like Callebaut, for the best results.

8 ounces white chocolate, chopped

7 tablespoons whipping cream

3 tablespoons butter

3 tablespoons fresh passion
  fruit juice (about 3 fruits)

⅓ cup pistachios, ground
  medium fine

3 tablespoons confectioners' sugar

4 ounces semi sweet
  chocolate, melted

Unsweetened cocoa powder

Place the white chocolate, whipping cream, and butter in a heatproof bowl set over a small pot of water. Gently heat over low heat, stirring on occasion, until the chocolate is fully melted. Remove from the heat, stir in the passion fruit juice, and pour the mixture into a glass loaf pan. Cool to room temperature, and then refrigerate the truffle filling for several hours up to overnight.

Scoop the truffles, using a melon baller dipped briefly in warm water (excess water shaken off), and place on a parchment-lined sheet pan. Refrigerate or freeze until firm. Meanwhile, combine the pistachios and confectioners' sugar in a small bowl. Shape each truffle by quickly rolling in the palm of your hand, then roll in the sugar mixture. Return the truffles to the tray and harden again for a few minutes.

Have your semi sweet chocolate melted and just warm. Place about 1 cup of the cocoa in a medium shallow dish or plastic container with lid (for later storage). Place a little of the melted chocolate on the palm of your hand, and quickly roll a nut-covered truffle into the chocolate. Drop the rolled truffle into the cocoa powder and give the container a quick shake, so that the truffle gets completely covered in cocoa. Repeat with the remaining truffles. Chill thoroughly before serving.

White chocolate doesn't firm up as much as dark chocolate and can be a little harder to work with, but don't give up. Truffles can be stored, covered, in the same container you roll them in with or without the extra cocoa, in the refrigerator or freezer, for at least a month, if not longer.

Widely grown in tropical regions, the passion fruit is round to oval in shape, either dark purple or yellow, with a soft, pulpy center and lots of seeds. In Hawaii, where the rich, tart juice is used to flavor sweet and savory dishes, it is called Liliko'i. To extract the juice from the fruit, press the flesh and seeds firmly through a sieve. Look for passion fruit in ethnic markets.

acknowledgments

I would like to say thank you to the team at Andrews McMeel who brought this book to fruition and for, once again, obliging my passion and vision, especially Kirsty Melville and Jean Lucas. And to Jean also for her tremendous patience and trust in my process. For my home team with gratitude to Carole Bidnick for championing this book from the start and believing in what I do; to Sara Remington for gorgeous, evocative photography and putting her heart and soul into each image; and to Lisa Berman for turning this book into a beautiful piece of art. I am very grateful to all of you.

Thanks also to friends, fellow writers, and food folks who have supported my writing and encouraged my path along the way, especially: Dianne Jacob, Sarah Henry, and Roberta Klugman. And others who fed me, shared a coffee or glass of wine, and otherwise spurred me on: Doug McKechnie, David Roe, Sukey Lilienthal, Nehama Weininger, Gwen Meyer, and Grace Harwood. And to Doug, also, for help with scanning images.

With appreciation to Borello Farms of Morgan Hill, California (grower of Blenheim apricots), for allowing us to spend the morning in their family's orchard during harvest. Thank you, Mark Pisoni, for connecting us. To the Chappellet family of St. Helena and Big Sur, for sharing their bounty of rangpur limes. And to Lyell Cash for offering his orchard and garden to photograph.

Thank you to my mom, brother, and sisters and their families for enriching my life, each in their own way. With particular thanks to my mom, Kim Rowe, for financial assistance at the start of this project, and to my sister Sara Rowe and Delic Tillman for opening their home to photo shoots and being supportive throughout. I am grateful to my little niece Chama for being a part of this book, and to my little cousin Lucy, for coming over to play and eating peach gelato. Thank you to Tina Snow and my cousin Winona Lewis for cheering me on and always lending an ear, and to my Aunt Dorcas for contributing props. To Mark Steele (no relation) for teaching me the art of fine desserts in the Sierra Mar kitchen, long ago. I'm also indebted to my stepmother Elena Steele, whose passion for good food and creativity in the kitchen has inspired me both as a cook and a writer.

Additionally, I want to express my appreciation for friends and *ohana* in Hawaii, especially Yana Deaton for her boundless generosity and *aloha* and for making me feel like I always have a home to return to. And to Joey Cabell, *mahalo*.

Plum Gorgeous could not have been written without my experiences in the orchard long ago and the urging of Kate Healey then and now; I am filled with gratitude for my years on Partington Ridge, for a friendship and connection to place that has endured. Lastly, thank you to my remarkable children, Trevor and Nicoya, who put up with my craziness while writing this book and who continue to inspire and awe me daily. I love you.

credits

With gratitude to the following copyright holders for permission to reprint:

Brief quotes from the Prologue (first page) and p. 168 from EPITAPH FOR A PEACH: FOUR SEASONS ON MY FAMILY FARM by David Mas Masumoto, copyright © 1995 by David Mas Masumoto. Reprinted by permission of HarperCollins Publishers.

Excerpt from A LITERATE PASSION: LETTERS OF ANAÏS NIN AND HENRY MILLER 1932-1953, copyright © 1987 by Rupert Pole, as Trustee under the Last Will and Testament of Anaïs Nin, reprinted by permission of Houghton Mifflin Harcourt Publishing Company.

From "Suzanne" by Leonard Cohen, from STRANGER MUSIC: SELECTED POEMS AND SONGS. Copyright © 1993 by Leonard Cohen Stranger Music, Inc. All rights reserved. Used by permission.

From LETTERS OF RAINER MARIA RILKE: 1892-1910 translated by Jane Bannard Greene and M. D. Herter Norton. Copyright © 1945 by W. W. Norton & Company, Inc., renewed © 1972 by M. C. Herter Norton. Used by permission of W. W. Norton & Company, Inc.

Excerpt "Nobody in the lane, and nothing, nothing but blackberries. . . ." from CROSSING THE WATER by Sylvia Plath, copyright © 1962 by Ted Hughes. This poem originally appeared in UNCOLLECTED POEMS, Turret Books, London, and in the Hudson Review. Reprinted by permission of HarperCollins Publishers.

"This Is Just to Say" by William Carlos Williams, from THE COLLECTED POEMS: VOLUME I, 1909-1939, copyright © 1938 by New Directions Publishing Corp. Reprinted by permission of New Directions Publishing Corp. In the UK/Commonwealth, from COLLECTED POEMS, Carcanet Press. Reprinted by permission of the publisher.

From "To The Poem" by Adonis, from SELECTED POEMS, translated by Khaled Mattawa, copyright © 2010 by Yale University Press. Reprinted by permission of Yale University Press.

OTHER ACKNOWLEDGMENTS

Translation for "The Oranges . . ." by Abd al-Rahman ibn Abi al-'Abbas (12th century) is unknown.

"To be happy . . ." by George Santayana, page ix, is quoted in the beginning of *The Gastronomical Me*, by MFK Fisher, original text is from *Egotism in German Philosophy* (1916).

"Rose is a rose is a rose is a rose" is from the poem *Sacred Emily* (1913), by Gertrude Stein, first printed in *Geography and Plays* (1922).

The handwritten script on page 107 is an excerpt from an old Cypriot Greek bridal song, first read in *Bitter Lemons* (1958) by Lawrence Durrell, in full as follows:

'Branches of orange, lovely with flowers;
Seven are the Bridesmaids who sew the bed.'
'Into the Bride's hall flew two nightingales;
They came to bring her English needles.'

metric conversions and equivalents

Metric Conversion Formulas

To Convert	Multiply
Ounces to grams	Ounces by 28.35
Pounds to kilograms	Pounds by .454
Teaspoons to milliliters	Teaspoons by 4.93
Tablespoons to milliliters	Tablespoons by 14.79
Fluid ounces to milliliters	Fluid ounces by 29.57
Cups to milliliters	Cups by 236.59
Cups to liters	Cups by .236
Pints to liters	Pints by .473
Quarts to liters	Quarts by .946
Gallons to liters	Gallons by 3.785
Inches to centimeters	Inches by 2.54

Approximate Metric Equivalents

Volume

¼ teaspoon	1 milliliter
½ teaspoon	2.5 milliliters
¾ teaspoon	4 milliliters
1 teaspoon	5 milliliters
1¼ teaspoon	6 milliliters
1½ teaspoon	7.5 milliliters
1¾ teaspoon	8.5 milliliters
2 teaspoons	10 milliliters
1 tablespoon (½ fluid ounce)	15 milliliters
2 tablespoons (1 fluid ounce)	30 milliliters
¼ cup	60 milliliters
⅓ cup	80 milliliters
½ cup (4 fluid ounces)	120 milliliters
⅔ cup	160 milliliters
¾ cup	180 milliliters
1 cup (8 fluid ounces)	240 milliliters
1¼ cups	300 milliliters
1½ cups (12 fluid ounces)	360 milliliters
1⅔ cups	400 milliliters
2 cups (1 pint)	460 milliliters
3 cups	700 milliliters
4 cups (1 quart)	0.95 liter
1 quart plus ¼ cup	1 liter
4 quarts (1 gallon)	3.8 liters

Weight

¼ ounce	7 grams
½ ounce	14 grams
¾ ounce	21 grams
1 ounce	28 grams
1¼ ounces	35 grams
1½ ounces	42.5 grams
1⅔ ounces	45 grams
2 ounces	57 grams
3 ounces	85 grams
4 ounces (¼ pound)	113 grams
5 ounces	142 grams
6 ounces	170 grams
7 ounces	198 grams
8 ounces (½ pound)	227 grams
16 ounces (1 pound)	454 grams
35.25 ounces (2.2 pounds)	1 kilogram

Length

⅛ inch	3 millimeters
¼ inch	6 millimeters
½ inch	1¼ centimeters
1 inch	2½ centimeters
2 inches	5 centimeters
2½ inches	6 centimeters
4 inches	10 centimeters
5 inches	13 centimeters
6 inches	15¼ centimeters
12 inches (1 foot)	30 centimeters

Oven Temperatures

To convert Fahrenheit to Celsius, subtract 32 from Fahrenheit, multiply the result by 5, then divide by 9.

Description	Fahrenheit	Celsius	British Gas Mark
Very cool	200°	95°	0
Very cool	225°	110°	¼
Very cool	250°	120°	½
Cool	275°	135°	1
Cool	300°	150°	2
Warm	325°	165°	3
Moderate	350°	175°	4
Moderately hot	375°	190°	5
Fairly hot	400°	200°	6
Hot	425°	220°	7
Very hot	450°	230°	8
Very hot	475°	245°	9

Information compiled from a variety of sources, including *Recipes into Type* by Joan Whitman and Dolores Simon (Newton, MA: Biscuit Books, 2000); *The New Food Lover's Companion* by Sharon Tyler Herbst (Hauppauge, NY: Barron's, 1995); and *Rosemary Brown's Big Kitchen Instruction Book* (Kansas City, MO: Andrews McMeel, 1998).

index